After Nativism

To Usha, Sam and Isla

For the light you shine

After Nativism

Belonging in an Age of Intolerance

Ash Amin

polity

Copyright © Ash Amin 2023

The right of Ash Amin to be identified as Author of this Work has been asserted in accordance with the UK Copyright, Designs and Patents Act 1988.

First published in 2023 by Polity Press

Polity Press
65 Bridge Street
Cambridge CB2 1UR, UK

Polity Press
111 River Street
Hoboken, NJ 07030, USA

All rights reserved. Except for the quotation of short passages for the purpose of criticism and review, no part of this publication may be reproduced, stored in a retrieval system or transmitted, in any form or by any means, electronic, mechanical, photocopying, recording or otherwise, without the prior permission of the publisher.

ISBN-13: 978-1-5095-5730-1
ISBN-13: 978-1-5095-5731-8(pb)

A catalogue record for this book is available from the British Library.

Library of Congress Control Number 2023931316

Typeset in 11 on 14pt Warnock Pro
by Cheshire Typesetting Ltd, Cuddington, Cheshire
Printed and bound by CPI Group (UK) Ltd, Croydon, CR0 4YY

The publisher has used its best endeavours to ensure that the URLs for external websites referred to in this book are correct and active at the time of going to press. However, the publisher has no responsibility for the websites and can make no guarantee that a site will remain live or that the content is or will remain appropriate.

Every effort has been made to trace all copyright holders, but if any have been overlooked the publisher will be pleased to include any necessary credits in any subsequent reprint or edition.

For further information on Polity, visit our website:
politybooks.com

Contents

Acknowledgements vi

Introduction 1
1. Grounds of Belonging 12
2. Street Affinities 51
3. The Intimate Public Sphere 97
4. Aesthetics of Nation 134
Coda 160

References 166
Index 190

Acknowledgements

This book has been written under the dark shadow of Covid-19. I started to write it in March 2020, shortly after returning from the field in Delhi. There followed many months of isolation in my cubbyhole at home, trying to grapple with ways of getting past the corrosions of nativist nationalism without losing my findings on the lives of slumdwellers and the homeless in Delhi. Thinking in isolation for so long was not easy, but I was helped by the opportunity to escape to Uppsala for three months in Summer 2021, and to Naples and Turin for five weeks in Spring 2022. I am enormously grateful to the Swedish Research Council for awarding me the 2021 Olof Palme Visiting Chair, which took me to Uppsala University, where my host Anders Ekström created the perfect environment for me to continue writing the book amid many stimulating conversations with him and his partner Marika Hedin, and at a seminar hosted by the Swedish Collegium for Advanced Study. For the Italian escape, I thank Giovanni Laino and Enrica Morlicchio for bringing me back to Naples, the city I love for its many inventions against aversion, and I thank Michele Lancione and Francesca Governa for gathering a stimulating body of young scholars in Turin to interrogate my ideas on the affordances of place. These ideas were greatly influenced by my month in Delhi just before lockdown examining the dwelling practices of the poor and their effects on subjectivity and sociality. Without the guidance of Maan Barua, Shaunak Sen and Gufran Alam, this inquiry would have faltered and I could not have hoped for a better assistant in the field than Gunjesh Kumar.

The writing was not always lonely and bewildering. I have benefited hugely from comments on parts of the book from Anders Ekström, Nigel Thrift, Michele Lancione, Maan Barua, Gunjesh Kumar, Colin McFarlane, Ravi Sundaram, Peter Phillimore, Veena Das, Tim Gardam, Patrick Wright, Isabel Airas, Maria Hagan and Philip Lewis. I am grateful to them all, as I am to attentive audiences at online and offline presentations in Naples, Turin, Rotterdam, Delhi, Uppsala, Stockholm, Tromsø and Cambridge. Two anonymous readers selected by Polity Press read the whole draft, one of whose stiff comments prompted me to rewrite the whole book after gentle but stern persuasion from John Thompson to offer a clear and original argument. I cannot judge if I have succeeded, but the criticisms and suggestions were invaluable. Finally, someone stuck with me during the isolation forced by the pandemic has been my partner Lynne Brown, who has had to suffer more than her fair share of doubts, irritability and absent presence. She has done so with patience and encouragement and my gratitude to her is immeasurable. There can be no denying, however, that the weight of the pandemic and the terrible times we live in has been hard to bear. This book offers a glimpse of how things could be different.

Introduction

What credible narrative and aesthetic of belonging could progressive forces mobilize to counteract today's sways of strongarm nationalism preying on popular animosities of secession and aversion? That is the question addressed in this book. Populations in the old and recent liberal democracies are turning in large numbers to a politics of native nation for reassurance against precarity, uncertainty and displacement. Think alone of developments in the last decade in the United States, the United Kingdom, Brazil, India, Poland, Hungary, France, Italy and Turkey, where across their differences in secular or religious nativist drift, a consensus has grown deriding elites, migrants, minorities, liberals, experts, professionals and cosmopolitans as the enemies of the nation. These figures are openly attacked on the street and in media and political life for corrupting the democratic process, sacrificing the national economy, destroying national cultural identity and social cohesion, and betraying the interests of a historic peoples. The developments are dangerous and punitive, with strong echoes of the animosities that culminated in the victories of fascism and Nazism in the early twentieth century. Today's discontents see the figures of suspicion as protagonists of a defunct liberal order that should be replaced by an illiberal one entrusted to a strong leadership ready to suppress dissent and constitutional legacies, tighten the boundaries of the nation, promote indigenous interests and communicate directly with the people. Across the countries named above, this leadership has got stronger and more organized, carried into government by the votes of hundreds of millions of people, or circling close to the corridors of power and influence.

In the ballot box and public opinion, the givens of liberal democracy are being tested by a politics of authoritarian nativism with its own affective and institutional machinery. As Jan Willem Duyvendak and Josip Kešić (2022) argue, liberal ideas are falling silent or themselves veering towards a discourse of deserving citizens and undeserving subjects in order to claim the ground of nativist populism. The slim victories of social democratic parties have the ring of liberalism surviving by virtue of just enough electoral fear of the consequences of xenophobic nationalism, not conviction in the plural, open and democratic society as the site of prosperity, wellbeing and security. It is ironic that the steady ascendancy of progressive attitudes over the decades recorded by social surveys, especially among younger and urban populations, towards consumerism, nature conservation, and sexual, cultural and personal liberty, is no proxy of popular conviction in liberal democracy as a political necessity and staple of national belonging. Perhaps this is because of a mounting perception that liberal democracy has betrayed the material interests, sense of place and voice of 'ordinary' citizens. But it is also because the progressive mainstream – liberal or social democratic – has lost its voice and verve, pushed by nativist populism towards a drawbridge politics of selective welfare, populist appeasement and border closure to secure its electoral survival. It has not responded by developing a clear and compelling narrative of the good society premised on the reciprocities of cosmopolitan engagement, generalized wellbeing and democratic expansion. It has not laid out an imaginary of what it means to belong beyond the strictures of closed national and historical community. In the gap, nativism has managed to insert nationalism and old-country traditions into the heart of popular understanding of the good society, untroubled by another counternarrative of belonging. It has made capital out of 'democracy fatigue' (Appadurai, 2019).

This book argues that disarming nativism will require more than assuring the material and existential security of the left-behind disenchanted with liberal democracy. The regeneration of distressed neighbourhoods, cities and regions, the fairer allocation of decent, secure and well-paid employment, the reduction of wealth, ownership and access disparities, and the removal of multiple deprivations faced by the disadvantaged through composites of welfare support covering basic income, educational, health, service and shelter needs, are all important elements of a political economy of social and spatial justice needed to dampen the discontentment feeding nativism. While recognizing the necessity of such a politics of social equity, this book's primary argument is that the lines of the future drawn by nativism are of an affective nature about imagined community, with questions of belonging and voice lying at the heart of popular perceptions of just dues. This is evident in the strained democracies in battles of identity appearing at the centre of putting America or the UK 'first' since the Trump years and the Brexit referendum, in Hungarian and Polish responses to the EU and liberalism discussed as matters of national autonomy and cultural heritage, and in debate in India on the country's prosperity and security posed in terms of the choice between Hindu nationalism and secular pluralism. Public senses of wellbeing have become closely intertwined with sentiments of imagined community, exactly in the ways theorized by Benedict Anderson, Ernest Gellner and Mark Billig for resurgences of nationalism in earlier times.

This is the territory that progressive forces – liberal, social democratic, socialist – need to reclaim so as to shift public sentiment away from xenophobic intolerance amid scarcity towards one of convivial coexistence and common effort amid shared risk and uncertainty, from which new understandings of belonging might settle. Building on relational ideas of belonging premised on the encounter (e.g. in the writings of Judith Butler and Marilyn Strathern) the book argues that progressives should develop a political imaginary of belonging projected from the ground of everyday negotiations of difference. A clear – and credible – alternative to defining community as the closed indigenous nation would be to press for a relational definition premised on the reality in modern nations of multiple and shifting geographies of encounter and affiliation (rather than to turn to benign forms of civic patriotism as anti-nationalist parties have tried, largely unsuccessfully). These geographies, for most people and places in the liberal democracies, turn out to be transnational, plural and evolving, as well as lived negotiations of distance and difference and not just of proximity and sameness stemming from long global histories of colonization, migration, travel, communication and consumption. A sense of nation – it is suggested – could be fostered from these geographies by recognizing constitutive plurality and difference and projecting community as the challenge of building a shared sense of place, common purpose and collaborative encounter amid the pluralities of belonging. There are many cultural crossings of the everyday that could be foregrounded as the measure of community and its cohesion, against nationalist mythologies of the homogeneous and autarchic nation. This is the first of three lines of argument in the book for a new politics of belonging.

The second relates to finding ways in the public sphere for 'common practice with others', to cite Isabelle Stengers (2015a), so that the trend facilitated by the digital media of vocalization in public from all social and spatial quarters can be harnessed for collective ends. Nativism, with its derision of experts, elites, professional politicians and bureaucracies, thrives on the fiction of direct communion between the people and their advocates; one sustained by a vastly expanded public sphere whose digital platforms inflate small communities and fringe concerns, amplify parallel worlds of opinion to the detriment of cross-dialogue and the general interest, and leave communities feeling connected, empowered and politically significant. Because it is unruly and fragmented, the public sphere does not – nor can it – exist as the arena in which democracy is enhanced through open and vigorous debate and healthy checks between delegated institutions and a civically minded citizenry, as envisaged by its pioneers such as Walter Lippmann, Hannah Arendt, Jürgen Habermas and Chantal Mouffe. Yet it remains all powerful and influential, key to political outcomes in the expressive society, and an important site of belonging based on the multitude of claims and attachments coursing through it. The book suggests that a progressive politics of belonging could seek to reinforce a neglected dimension of the modern public sphere, which Anders Ekström (2021) describes as its legacy of publicness oriented towards the common interest. Backed by strident reforms to curb the power and influence of platform providers as well as to outlaw violent and hateful speech, the public sphere could be rebuilt as a meeting place where multiple forms of expertise and intelligence – professional and lay, expert and experiential – come together to address matters of common concern. The collaborations struck between professionals, communities, experts and decision makers during the Covid-19 pandemic are a good example of such publicness, as are experiments of living with or mitigating the climate crisis through collaborations across spatial and epistemic boundaries. A culture of publicness building as a form of belonging would begin to neutralize the war of small worlds and corruptions of democratic debate typical of the digital public sphere of centrifugal animosities.

The book's third line of argument, following writing on how popular sentiments of belonging form in enactments of myths of nation, is to urge progressives to build an aesthetics of imagined community from the cultural conciliations of lived experience. Nativism's strength derives from its raw imagery of good insiders and bad outsiders, homely pasts and scary futures, secure traditions and disruptive invasions giving affective expression and energy to the misgivings of populations feeling entitled but betrayed. Its resurgence in the liberal and illiberal democracies has been greatly facilitated by a powerful archive of sounds and images of homely nation, proud tradition, secure borders and sovereign citizens. Nativism's opponents find themselves on the back foot, unable to muster popular support for a counter-aesthetics of belonging celebrating individual rights, democracy and the law, modernity and cosmopolitanism, or varieties of civic or moral patriotism. Sceptical of the chances of such an aesthetics of nation, the book proposes a more organic and syncretic aesthetics composed of arts publicizing the ongoing history of border crossings of all kinds making life and community. It suggests that anti-nativists should work at making visible and enchanting the archive of affirmative practices of coexistence, past and present, that expose the flimsiness of an aesthetics of national purity and isolation. Pursued as a dissident aesthetics for a new kind of society in exactly the same way as the nativist cause has successfully presented its mission, they could turn to diverse art forms to give form to the many practices of convivial coexistence, fugitive cohabitation and compassionate susceptibility that can be found among strangers, to the provisions of the shared infrastructural, natural and social commons that enable collective survival, and to the chains of formative connection across national, social and ecological boundaries whose severance weakens the human stock wherever located. Importantly, like past times of radical cause such as the nascent feminist, anti-colonial and labour movements with their distinctive iconography, progressives could develop a political aesthetic intended to move hearts and minds, moving on from tired repetition of the nostra of liberal or social democracy. Scanning our times, there are lessons to be learnt from the world environmental campaign's efforts to mount a media aesthetic that has proved highly effective in altering public opinion and sentiment. In this third argument for a new politics of belonging, the book makes no pretence of subalterns vanquishing hegemons, only the assumption that as public feeling grows for the myriad forms of coexistence and kinship within and between the species, nativist imagery of secessionist indigeneity will make less and less sense to people.

The book is organized into four chapters. The first chapter opens with a pen portrait of nativist developments across the old and new democracies. The aim is not to compare the varieties of strongarm nationalism, nor to provide anything like a comprehensive coverage, but to exemplify their commonalities of imagined nation and the threat posed by them to the legacy of liberal nation. The main body of the chapter sets out a counter-narrative of belonging for progressive movements to pursue based on making more of everyday negotiations of difference in urban neighbourhoods that contradict nativist fictions of conflict, and mobilizing a discourse of imagined nation as confluence of multiple relational geographies, opportunity of contiguous diversity and difference, and commons of civic engagement. While of such a cultural politics of belonging, the chapter accepts that any weakening of popular support for nativism also requires a political economy committed to generalized wellbeing and reduced inequality, the traces of which are provided in the conclusion of the book.

The second chapter, building on urban negotiations of difference and commonality portrayed in chapter 1, turns to the challenges of belonging posed by conditions of poverty, rudimentary infrastructures and a divisive biopolitical environment. Drawing on field evidence in an informal settlement and among the homeless in Delhi, the chapter examines subject positions and social relations challenged by harsh material circumstances making for resentment and abjection, overshadowed by a divisive Hindu nationalist politics pitting citizens against each other through clamorous declarations of the values, traditions and subjects that count and those that do not, such as secularism, cultural mixture, the inactive and Muslims. The chapter shows how cutting across these circumstances there are important mediations of place – ecological, infrastructural and institutional – that intervene in shaping the wellbeing and sense of belonging of the poor. These include fragile bridges of welfare and mutuality formed amid marginality through neighbourly exchanges, emergent infrastructures and services, shared place attachments and accommodations of spatial density. Such mediations, evident in the informal settlement in South Delhi, are absent in the inhospitable open spaces of Old Delhi where the homeless camp out, their fortunes and outlooks shielded from national conjugations of imagined community only through the protections offered by a stretched network of charities and non-governmental organizations (NGOs).

The third chapter takes up the politics of voice at the heart of nativist complaint about the elitist exclusions of liberal democracy leaving majorities feeling like strangers in their own land. While one obvious option for progressive forces is to make the people's voice the gauge of a functioning polity by strengthening direct and participatory democracy, ensuring greater political transparency and accountability, and working to decentre power to multi-stakeholder regional assemblies, the chapter chooses to focus on the (digital) public sphere, because of its enormous contemporary significance as an arena of popular participation and site of nativist mobilization. It sees the public sphere as pivotal to perceptions of imagined community and as tightly woven into the political arena. The chapter sets out its case and steps for strengthening in the public sphere dispositions of publicness, shared interest and care for the commons, after discussing the difficulties of harnessing the principles of rational or agonistic deliberation, and the possibilities for regulating its digital platforms and infrastructures against malfeasance. While the case for a politics of publicness is made without any assumptions of guaranteeing the progressive cause, it is considered essential for strengthening a culture of collective orientation in a public sphere that has become powerful and ubiquitous.

The fourth chapter lays out its argument for a new aesthetics of imagined community. It summarizes the visual and sentimental biases working in favour of a politics of nation premised on the return of a golden age of proud indigeneity, and explains why an existing counter-aesthetic of republican, cosmopolitan or civic nation will not succeed in matching the power of the nativist aesthetic. It outlines another course giving expressive form and rhetorical energy to the long archive of everyday border crossings, distant connections and collective orientations that make identities but remain neglected in narratives of nation. The case is made for a minor aesthetics of belonging that makes visible relational connections in the undergrowth of cultural life, in the process weakening the hold of nativist myths of imagined community and giving aesthetic momentum to the realities of plural nation.

In a short conclusion, the book looks past its proposed narrative of belonging premised on the relation, to a political economy of managed markets, welfare equality and social inclusion able to underwrite the lives and livelihoods of the left-behind in ways that temper aversion and resentment. Here the book joins progressive arguments pressing for meaningful interventions to ensure welfare parity, equality of opportunity and economic redistribution, stop the spread of falsehoods, hate and harm, counteract easy scapegoating and unfounded claims, democratize and decentralize political and economic power and place professional and lay expertise and intelligence in collaborative dialogue. Its distinctiveness, however, lies in propositions of belonging able to rework public understanding of imagined community, social coexistence and public encounter, exposing claims of foreign contamination, lost sovereignty and cultural dilution as the hype of shadowy forces advancing their own interests at the expense of the democratic and convivial. The propositions are not offered from an empty ground but from interactions that already exist in the prosaic doings of infrastructures and services, collective welfare programmes, neighbourhood and municipal initiatives, encounters in public space, existential affinities with unknown others, including nonhumans, and countless collaborations in schools, workplaces, places of worship, clubs and associations. In presenting community as a yet to be made boundary crossing with others to collectively face an uncertain future, the book's aim is to dislodge the staging of nation as identity drama.

If the book reads as a polemic, it is to encourage a new politics of imagined community able to channel the social furies and displacements of our times away from nativist regressions riddled with animosity towards the plural and open society. In the absence of a clear and compelling counter-aesthetic of nation, many of the struggles of class, gender, sexual, racial and postcolonial freedom and equity won over the last half century risk being eroded, left without affective momentum and ideational unity, anachronized by the drumbeat of nativist nationalism. This is already happening, evident in popular endorsement of nativist dismissal of the achievements of liberal and social democracy as disunifying and counter-progressive, against the strong and proud nation. So, the book's polemical tone arises from an acute sense of urgency to safeguard hard-won protections of social justice, cultural freedom and political inclusion. In laying out new terms of belonging, however, the book stops short of discussing their delivery, not only because of important differences of nativist and progressive confrontation and organization in the democracies under strain, but also because it is hard to identify the prime movers given widespread official liberal and social democratic silence towards the cultural politics of nativism. Echoing Rebecca Solnit's argument (2021) that hope amid alarming political neglect to tackle the climate emergency may lie in the ability of people around the world as demanding citizens and organizers of counter-experiments to force the official centres of power to act, an imaginary of belonging based on tangible relational practices and affects may play its part in waking up the stupefied centres of politics.

1
Grounds of Belonging

Introduction

This is not a safe time to be a secular liberal or foreigner in many European countries, and for that matter, in other democracies such as the US, Turkey, India and Brazil, upended by nativist nationalism. After enduring long periods of austerity, rising inequality and welfare austerity, majorities in the old and new democracies are sensing a moving cast of subjects as the enemies of the nation, a threat to collective wellbeing, identity and autonomy. Persuaded by swashbuckling nativists such as Trump, Orbán, Erdoğan, Meloni, Le Pen and Bolsonaro to be the deserving 'somewheres' whose future has been stolen by deracinated 'anywheres', majorities feeling left behind are seeking salvation in the return of the homely and indigenous nation protected by the autarchic state. They have been convinced by nationalists that the removal of the discrepant is required to preserve self and community, its meaning kept conveniently malleable to include immigration, cultural pluralism, international federation, liberalism, experts, elites and even germs as the true sources of national problems such as poverty and inequality, social and regional division, cultural disunity and political weakness. The simple repetition of the associations seems to suffice as proof, straight out of the playbook of past ethno-nationalist attacks on particular subjects and cultural orientations. Like them, nativists and their publics find themselves busily justifying the 'unpleasantness' of xenophobia, border controls and identity checks as an imperative of national salvation returning sovereignty to a neglected people. By sleight of hand many unsubstantiated connections are being made, with devastating consequences for those identified as threats, from migrants and minorities to liberals and cosmopolitans.

This story of recovered sovereignty is proving popular to disgruntled citizens because it promises a political settlement working directly for the 'people', cleared – in some understandings – of the impediments of liberal democracy, including the parliamentary process, an independent judiciary, a critical press and free debate. It offers the charm of a popular democracy of direct communion between a historical population and a post-political cadre of rough, tough, charismatic individuals fired by patriotic fervour. The bitter irony is that in the name of popular democracy is proposed a demagoguery tearing into representative politics, legal and expert authority and democratic discussion, and into a raft of subjects and citizens tarnished as threats and misfits. It is true that the tonalities and intensities of nativist nationalism in Europe and beyond are far from uniform. Its reach into the political life of different countries is varied, as is the strength of its commitment to illiberalism and its incorporation into government. But it is disturbingly uniform in its aversion to migrants, refugees and minorities, with public and political discourse in the democracies obsessing about migration numbers, the motives and rights of refugees and the loyalties of migrants and minorities, quick to declare limits to national carrying capacity and the mixture of identities and cultures. It is uniform in its nostalgia for a mighty and mythic past free of non-indigenous peoples and traditions, and its contempt for the modern in its various guises, including science and expertise, liberal and deliberative democracy, legal, constitutional and bureaucratic conventions, the educated, professional and cosmopolitan sections of society, and elites, financiers and 'big business' accused of siphoning off riches and opportunities. It is uniform in its commitment to a politics of wild fabrications, moral outrage and violence towards those people and precepts that stand in the way of strongarm nationalism, its shock troops ready to tear down the ways of liberal democracy.

These are some of the common threads between otherwise distinctive forms of nationalist rebirth with their particular grievances, declared enemies and invocations of lost legacies of greatness. In Brazil, Bolsonaro's populist momentum preyed on anger against a past of metropolitan bias, slum and countryside poverty, socialist leanings and government and industrial corruption, while Trump's megaphone of Making America Great Again finds ears among the disenchanted working classes, upcountry evangelists and old settlers told to have been betrayed by open borders, the liberal establishment and the erosion of White power. In Poland and Hungary, the far right, firmly ensconced in government, makes a virtue of illiberal democracy, quick to impose curbs on free speech, the law and constitutional freedoms won after the collapse of state socialism, endorsed by a hard-done-by population promised the greatness and security of past times of resistance against the invasions of conquerors, communists, non-Christians and market modernizers. In a spectacular reversal of India's post-independence commitment to secular democracy and the plural nation, the Modi government and its Hindu nationalist cadres, spread in every nook of the state apparatus, public sphere and civil society, have shifted popular understanding of belonging as a battle between rightful Hindus and wronging Muslims, the deserving poor and usurping elites and intellectuals, and precolonial wisdoms and Western corruptions.

The turnaround has won the support of hundreds of millions of Hindu slumdwellers, rural poor, manual workers, urban middle classes and businesses seeing new opportunities in the cleansed nation. In France, the republican nationalism of Le Pen has gradually grown into a nationwide movement supported by a substantial proportion of the electorate demanding immigration controls, freedom from the EU, a better deal for the white working class and derecognition of Islam and France's Muslim heritage. The aggressive nationalism of Salvini and Meloni in Italy is no different, expect perhaps in its more veiled defence of republicanism to appease the Catholic population and in its recourse to a fiction of national greatness anticipated by Mussolini's fascists. In the UK, the nativism unlocked by the Brexit referendum is driven by an English nationalism feeding on colonial fantasies of grandeur, island isolationism and disenchantment among many communities left behind by exclusions of work, welfare, income and voice in recent decades, interpreted by the Right as the product of the unregulated economy, EU membership, immigration and elite power.

These nativist campaigns draw on distinctive histories of grievance and redemption, yet after their growing collaborations and shared international platforms (Shroufi, 2015), their rants against liberal democracy and the open society and their versions of strongarm nationalism and popular sovereignty increasingly look the same. They project the same image of the sequestered and cohesive nation and they share an oiled machinery of hate and nostalgia to build popular momentum behind their cause (Mishra, 2017). They act as though behind them blow the winds of change through democracies troubled by globalization, austerity and inequality. Into this century, they have secured considerable electoral success and traction in popular political culture, unruffled by moments of electoral defeat, whether Le Pen's in France, Trump's in the US or Bolsonaro's in Brazil. Echoing past campaigns turning mass disaffection into hope through loose and caustic associations, aggrieved majorities are seeing nativism as the bearer of prosperity and wellbeing, casting social democracy, liberalism and cosmopolitanism as the sources of social misery and national decline (Connolly, 2017; Hochschild, 2018). In or out of power, nativist nationalism has found its momentum, telling people who believe themselves to be hard-done-by indigenes that their identity and sovereignty has been stolen by migrants, minorities and cosmopolitans, in enacting a national drama staging majorities as victims and these others as perpetrators and then promising unity and stability through the bonds of tradition, cultural homogeneity and homeland welfare. It has returned the politics of imagined community to the centre of national conversations on almost everything, ranging from questions of identity, cohesion and belonging, to those relating to the political economy of prosperity and security, and the character of state sovereignty and the democratic society. The tones of national identity have become the passing point of public discussion on the big matters of statehood, citizenship and wellbeing.

In this discussion, noticeably absent has been the offer of a counter-narrative of belonging that offers compelling reasons to protect the open, deliberative and cosmopolitan society, or indeed, any other alternative to the nativist imaginary of nation. Blinded by the thymotic rage and wild claims of nativism, paralysed by the surge of popular support for it, and reticent to enter a public discussion of national identity so dominated by ethno-nationalists, progressives have tended to shy away from this terrain. Their reaction to the predicaments of the left-behind and disaffected, and to the drumbeat of homeland protectionism and cultural preservation, has been to look to take the sting out of nationalism by improving the material circumstances of communities drawn to it. They have tended to turn to a politics of social inclusion and national cohesion based on public investment and community empowerment programmes, improved income and welfare support for those less well-off and at a disadvantage, and redistributive measures of various kinds to reduce inequality (without addressing its causes in the free reign of markets, as suggested later in this chapter), while muttering in their collar about the positives of patriotism and keeping quiet about the benefits of multiculturalism and internationalism. There has been little effort to mount a strong counter-culture of belonging and sovereignty to nativism. For example, in the name of a fairer and more equitable society, the British Labour Party produced an election manifesto in 2019 replete with interventions to step up public ownership, regulate the economy, redistribute wealth, reduce regional and social inequality and maintain international connections, but left the electorate none the wiser about the vision of the good life on offer. Perhaps the Party was too scared to broach the delicate question of imagined community in a turbocharged Brexit environment and, indeed, a tide of English nationalism swept the Conservatives into power once more.

But this is not an isolated example. The absence of a counter-narrative of belonging is evident in other countries with nativists in government or enjoying popular support. Elsewhere in Europe, progressives have acquiesced to nationalist fervour against immigration, universal welfare and cultural pluralism, while defending modest green and redistributive measures within a pro-corporate neoliberal political economy. This has happened along the arc of countries sweeping north of the western Mediterranean through Germany and the Benelux countries to the Scandinavian region. Meanwhile, more ambitious parties such as Syriza in Greece and Podemos in Spain, which tried to confront austerity, negligent government, xenophobic aversion and market rule through a combination of expansionary, pro-poor and inclusive government policies, failed to find lasting traction, faced off by the Right and the political mainstream but also hostile vested economic interests and a suspicious European Union. Their sketches of social populism and participatory democracy fell short of securing the material and existential securities needed to sustain its willing public. In Poland and Hungary, the weak and fragmented opposition to the self-declared illiberal nationalists in power, who have radically altered the institutional and cultural landscape to keep themselves in government with the support of homeland traditionalists and cultural conservatives, has struggled to articulate a vision of the open and inclusive society free of the tarnish of being derived from a European liberal model considered neglectful of its weakest members and inconsistent with past collective traditions. In India, the political opposition, crushed by Hindu fundamentalism, the cult of money and muscular aggressivity, has found it hard to re-enchant its post-independence tradition of Gandhian tolerance and secularism to hold together a vast and plural nation. In the US, the Democrats won the presidential election in 2020, but, with the Trump nativists poised, have failed to recover the common American dream that works through its migrant legacy, a capacious model of universal welfare, or the colours of a post-racial state.

The pandemic has unmasked the incompetence, fakery and ignorance of nativist regimes whose inactions and denials have escalated the death toll and who offer no route out of the expected economic downturn. The Trump and Bolsonaro regimes are a case in point. Equally, public support for universal welfare will weaken once the competitive pressures of surviving the recession start to bite, pitting communities against each other, unless tangible social protections are accompanied by a convincing narrative of national wellbeing based on generalized welfare, commonality and international reciprocity. It is revealing that the unprecedented decision in July 2020 by a parsimonious EU to establish a fund to help member states recover from the pandemic, along with the generous furlough provisions and health protections rolled out by some states, have been presented as crisis measures and not as the makings of a new, welfarist, political economy. The will to name a new course between neoliberalism and nativism has been lacking, which could prove to be costly. In the immediate aftermath of the 2007 financial crisis, it was widely accepted that the crisis would require radical reform and regulation of banking, along with significant state shoring up of consumption to avoid world economic collapse. There was talk of ending neoliberalism, yet no clear script of the new emerged, allowing old vested interests to deride 'quantitative easing' as a liberal folly and push for austerity measures that have prolonged the recession into the present, suffocating many vulnerable economies and lives. Barely any regulation of finance, industry and commerce followed, allowing elites, corporations and oligarchies to regroup, while millions languished in the gig economy, unemployment, poverty and social exclusion. In the political jostle to code the recession, the 'left-behind' found more solace in impassioned nativist derision of experts, elites, immigrants, globalization and remote politicians than in mute social democratic arguments for tighter economic regulation and welfare expansion. In the meantime, from the sidelines, the corporate beneficiaries of neoliberalism looked on unscathed, happy to shield behind nativist distractions leaving them free to roam.

The salient point is that there will be no easy translation of the ethic of care built during the pandemic into public demand for the inclusive welfare society without active political advocacy for its necessity and value. The overlaps of nativism and neoliberalism struck during the decade of austerity (Monbiot, 2017; Connolly, 2019) conspire to cast the pandemic as reason to reopen the economy at any cost, including the gig economy that leaves its vulnerable subjects exposed; to champion libertarian freedoms while coming down hard on unwanted subjects such as refugees and migrants now cast as biosecurity threats; to claim as their own state interventions once associated with social democracy; and to close down opposition and dissent on grounds of emergency management. Nativist bluster may have rung hollow during the pandemic, but without affecting its slippery tricks to turn tragedy to its own advantage as shown in the United Kingdom, Poland and Hungary. The political impetus for an ethic of universal care will survive only if part of a wider campaign for a different and more convivial social order, invested with urgency, desirability and tangibility.

This is the argument of the chapter, claiming that the anxieties of the disenchanted drawn to nativism are of the lifeworld and how it is felt and framed. These are anxieties of material lack and insecurity requiring a political economy of distributed investments, stepped-up market regulations and welfare protections (illustrated in the concluding section for European democracies), but they also express resentments of cultural displacement that material improvements will only partially allay. They beckon towards a politics of belonging that accepts grassroot demands for recognition without ceding the narrative of nation to indigeneity and cultural homogeneity by showing that the open, plural and shared nation poses no threat, and is already customary in mainstream cultural practice. While nativism is quick to interpret the left-behind as the abandoned white working classes so as to justify a thinly veiled colonial politics of racial and class purification, an abundant body of research summarized in the next section shows their identities to be plural and evolving, their curiosities and affiliations to be translocal and transcultural, and their concerns shared with others across the social spectrum, including migrants and minorities. This ground of shared concerns, multiple identities and plural geographies of attachment enables the pursuit of inclusive welfare to be nested within a narrative of heterogenous and evolving national identity, to reveal the vacuity of arguments pitting deserving 'somewheres' against deracinated 'anywheres' (Goodhart, 2017). It makes for a politics of narrating the nation as a connective commons and zone of encounter amid constitutive difference and many geographies of attachment. It makes, as elaborated in the second section, for a politics of civic nation, allowing progressive forces to look beyond the strictures of nationalism or patriotism to publicly define and defend community and belonging as a challenge of shared coexistence.

Nativism thrives on claiming that the 'people' have been abandoned by a detached liberal or social democracy serving elite and 'anywhere' interests. It demands a politics that speaks directly to and for the 'people', in its strongarm version jettisoning parliamentary sovereignty, the civic service and judiciary, and the critical media, as shown by government actions in India, Brazil, the UK, Poland and Hungary. It seeks to replace parliamentary democracy with a political cadre supposedly in dialogue with the suppressed native population, tearing into representative politics, legal and expert authority, and free and rational debate. Its claim upon 'direct democracy' resonates with the disenchanted and left-behind. The chapter opens an argument in the book that a counter-politics should focus on unmasking the violence and betrayals of demagogic populism instead of staying with the current inclination to appease the 'left-behind', pronounce against migrants, claim the cloak of patriotism and acquiesce to neoliberal power. It could address popular antipathy to elite, remote and tokenistic government, not by defending the liberal status quo, but by campaigning to democratize power through open and transparent government, decentralize authority to civic organizations, workplaces, communities and regions, enjoin vernacular, professional and delegated expertise, and encourage genuine public debate and deliberation. Social democracy could commit to its own radical expansion, convinced that in this authoritarian moment the way forward lies in expanding democratic representation and participation, tackling the uncertain future collaboratively and not through retreat into a fictive past (Bryant and Knight, 2019).

Lived Identities, Imagined Community

In plural societies the swings between public empathy, indifference and antipathy towards migrants and minorities tend to be fluid, but harden when singular discourses of imagined community work their way into the cultural foreground. A prequel to this book (Amin, 2012) proposed seeing the swings as mediated by the play between rhythms of daily interaction – physical and virtual – influenced by factors such as personal inclination and the quality of encounter, and framings of difference within national narratives of belonging, the biopolitics of population management and legal and institutional understandings of citizenship. Through this lens, the shift in many democracies from national framings of community that concealed the discriminations of race, colony and class under propositions of universal individual and collective rights, towards ethnonationalist framings that presume and prey on these discriminations, can be seen as affectively influencing everyday accommodations of diversity and difference. Taking advantage of austerity's maldistributions of parsimonious work, welfare and security, the nativist narrative of nation as the preserve of an indigenous community and its historic traditions is seeping into an everyday unconscious in which majorities reimagine migrants and minorities as outsiders rather than as co-citizens. This is not happening uniformly, with the autonomies of everyday encounter continuing to persist in joint experience, shared space, serendipitous encounter, shared interests and other examples of coming together in specific micropublics (Darling and Wilson, 2016; Wise, 2016). But they do so against the grain and in the shadow of an ascendant biopolitics of aversion to misfits, migrants and minorities that considers them out of place.

Yet the micropublics are far from exceptional, even among people and places held to be 'somewheres' content among their own kind and moored traditions, and suspicious of diversity and change. The evidence from a body of urban ethnographies of mixed and white working-class neighbourhoods confronted by austerity, migration and cultural change paints a picture of anxiety, rootedness and intolerance mingled with a sense of shared space, common experience and openness to change. These contrasting tendencies are found among individuals and their social networks, including those persuaded by nativist discourse, and across divisions of socio-economic status, race and ethnicity, and settlement history, their balance shaped in personal histories of mobility and experience. They are not confined to a particular social group, for example, more worldly white nativists. This is not surprising, given the multiple and evolving character of identity and attachment resulting from intensive contemporary experience of consumption, travel, education, work, leisure and encounter, and also the extensive reshaping of cities and regions by modernity's migrations, distant influences and trans-local connections and networks, making for a sense of place as relationally and globally constituted, despite the prim fantasies of nostalgic localists (Massey, 2005). Typically, in his ethnography of working-class Peterborough that has undergone considerable change in the last decade due to migration and the hardships of austerity, Ben Rogaly (2020) shows how its settled residents and East European and South Asian migrants have been on the giving or receiving end of racism and xenophobia, but also shared similar histories of mobility and attachments to place, an ease with difference and convivial exchanges in the city's workplaces and public spaces. Through painstaking groundwork in supposedly left-behind places, Rogaly's ten-year study gets behind political and media slogans of irreconcilable difference and traduced ways of life, to disclose disturbing escalations of hardship, insecurity and xenophobia or racism during a time of persistent austerity and anti-migrant sentiment, which, however, do not conform to predictable class and ethnic stereotypes. It also finds ample evidence of interpersonal connections, cosmopolitan practices and place attachments within an ethnically and durationally differentiated working class that are not supposed to prevail in the worlds of 'left-behind somewheres'. These nuances exist also within 'white flight' areas more explicitly against immigration, elites and 'Europe', as we discover from Patrick Wright's (2020) intergenerational study of the Isle of Sheppey in Kent that voted strongly in favour of Brexit but not as a little England yearning for pre-immigration 'old ways', from Anoop Nayak's (2003) work on white masculinities in Northern England hardened by deindustrialization and neglect, and from Joe Kennedy's (2018) exposure of the authenticity of the white British working class. The 'subaltern cosmopolitanism' of these areas may be more 'inward-oriented' (Zeng, 2014) and veer towards reassurances of the familiar within known territory, but it also includes many of the crossings identified by Rogaly.

Zeng positions the subaltern cosmopolitanism of migrants and minorities in Europe as more 'outward-oriented', spurred by honed agilities and situated adjustments learned to negotiate existential challenges and discriminations encountered in home and host societies. Here, too, the evidence strays far from the caricature clumsily cobbled together from anecdotes and extreme examples, portraying refugees, economic migrants, less well-off ethnic minorities and religious communities such as Muslims as culturally closed, unable or unwilling to integrate, locked amongst their own and faraway diasporas and places, only concerned with scavenging what they can. In the caricature, these are people whose 'somewheres' are in other lands or in sealed-off local enclaves, where few loyalties to and ties with the host nation are to be found. They are judged to be intruders, out of place. The ethnographies, following the trajectories of particular individuals or neighbourhoods, tell a different story: one of plural identities, connections and loyalties acquired in the course of moving internationally and nationally, fending off discrimination and exclusion, finding the means to survive and flourish, and cultivating a sense of home and belonging. The pluralities are shown to cross social, cultural and territorial boundaries, combine customary ties and loyalties (often in order to survive alienation and hostility) with new affiliations acquired in the journey through education and work and consumption and leisure, and include affinities with the people and places of arrival and settlement. The subjects emerge as people with rich histories and evolving lives, with a sense of home and belonging that is simultaneously diasporic and situated, loyal to place and nation in cultivated ways that many 'natives' are not in their taken-for-granted citizenship. The ethnographies sketch biographies of experience, affiliation and desire that contain so much more than in the staid habit of reducing the subjectivity and rights of migrants and minorities in Europe to superficial 'identity' categories.

This is well illustrated in Les Back and Shamser Sinha's (2018) study of young adult migrants negotiating London since the 2008 financial crisis: the heightened economic precarities and insecure conditions of work, the invasive surveillance from a Conservative-led regime of hostile management of migration, and the racism and xenophobia unleashed during and after the Brexit referendum in 2016. A rare care for method, incorporating interviews, diaries, poems, stories, sketches and photographs, along with long-term contact with the research subjects, makes room for the voices of the migrants to be heard, provides the opening for a fuller understanding of the trajectories and everyday lives of the migrants. Afforded the dignity of recognition and expression, the 'migrants' emerge as gentle, capable and aspiring citizens who have run the gauntlet of arduous or dangerous migration journeys, poor and erratic work and welfare opportunities in the undergrowth of the informal or illegal economy, a border regime making it harder and harder to stay and asking institutions and the public to report suspected illegal migrants, and unapologetic hostility and racism from a rekindled colonial nationalism averse to the subjects of Empire and 'opportunists' from Europe. Back and Sinha's interlocutors, marked by these trials and indignities, speak of adjusting and learning from being on the move and dislocated, living across borders and developing a sense of home through intimacies in dispersed places, times and communities, and wondering why there is no recognition that they are in the UK because of its colonial past or its current geopolitical interventions (e.g. in the Middle East), forever waiting to be allowed to stay, to not be monitored, to leave the ranks of the newest arrivals labelled as the unwanted even by others from migrant backgrounds. But the narratives are offered without rancour or reproach, and from a vantage point of adjusted life in the quest for settlement and contribution to city and nation. Through the discriminations and surveillances, we see forged practices of everyday inhabitation built around empathies with other Londoners encountered, care for the spaces dwelt in or regularly visited, rituals shared with others through work, education and social gatherings, curiosity for the new, refusal to be tainted by hatred and resentment, and a sense of the city made of mobilities and global connections shared with many others. In the detail of their lives, the migrants emerge as perpetually troubled by colonialism, racism and exclusionary border politics, but still willing members of the wider social fabric, aspiring settlers, home-makers and citizens, subjects determined to make their own way, 'ordinary' residents engaged in local ways of life. Other urban ethnographies confirm this portrait of fragile and tested belonging, including Suzi Hall's (2018, 2021) work on migrant street entrepreneurs in Manchester, Bristol, Birmingham, Leicester and South

London, Anoop Nayak's (2017) study of young Bangladeshi women in Sunderland and Sivamohan Valluvan's (2019) research with young working-class adults from minority backgrounds in London.

The lives disclosed by the ethnographies are completely at odds with the rhetorical construction, with powerful consequences, of migrants as dangerous and incompatible outsiders in Europe. It holds only without any knowledge of and interest in migrant lives, which turn out to be fragile, violated and part of the ordinary mix of the plural society. The pronouncements from on high can be condescending, even from reputedly sympathetic sources, including Slavoj Žižek declaring in the *London Review of Books* in 2015 that refugees

> should be reassured of their safety, but it should also be made clear to them that they have to accept the area of living allocated to them by European authorities, plus they have to respect the laws and social norms of European states. Yes, such a set of rules privileges the Western European way of life, but it is a price for European hospitality. These rules should be clearly stated and enforced, by repressive measures (against foreign fundamentalists as well as against our own anti-immigrant racists) if necessary.

In one sentence, the refugee is cast as the invasive subject, the outsider with different norms in need of repurposing, while Europe is projected as under threat, without any 'legal and moral responsibility for the consequences of colonial exploitation', an 'idealized phantasy, made possible by splitting it from unwanted aspects of identity' (Kulicka, 2017: 267, 274) conveniently cloaked around the unwanted intruder. Almost always, in casting the intruding figure as non-European, there enters a racial distinction with immediate affective power of white Europe with its own traditions confronted by yet more non-white people with other ways. The racial tag is rarely acknowledged, concealed under strenuous effort among stakeholders in the status quo to frame the problem as one of carrying capacity and cultural incompatibility. This sleight requires public discussion of 'why, and how exactly, has Europe so deftly managed to convert the precarious lives (and bodies) of migrants and refugees – disproportionately racialized as not-white, and in fact inordinately racialized as Black – into overtly de-racialized "migrant" lives' (De Genova, 2018: 1767). It requires asking if 'circumstances conspire to ensure that these lives truly do not matter – that these migrant lives are rendered utterly disposable – does it not seem plausible, if not probable, that race has something to do with it?' (De Genova, 2018: 1767).

The daily struggles of migrants and minorities to make a life for themselves, just like others sharing the same turf, need to enter the vocabulary of imagined community to challenge entrenched colour-coded reflexes of belonging further reinforced by nativist nationalism. Much needs to be acknowledged from the ground of daily experience, for example, the inclinations of young male Moroccans in Madrid and Bangladeshis in London towards their Muslim or country origins in the face of hostility towards them as 'immigrants', while maintaining pluralist, secular and Western lifestyles as residents of countries they feel part of (Gest, 2015). Or the territorial affinities shared by young adults in Brussels from different ethnic and class backgrounds who identify with the city and not nation or Europe as the space of 'we-feelings' (Elias, 2010), revealing the strength of sentiments of the shared lifeworld over those of imagined community (Delmotte et al., 2017). Or the character of refugee journeys across turbulent spaces of extortion, violence, slavery, imprisonment and extreme hardship, expressing a subjectivity of 'humanity, resilience, endurance, courage, and strategic decision making' (Press, 2017: 22) at odds with nativist caricature of the opportunist asylum seekers.

Such examples propose identity and belonging as relational practice and existential adjustment, as shown by Camilla Hawthorne (2017) in her study of African Italians 'exploring the possibilities of a new kind of hyphenated identity' (p. 158) through public art forms enabling their lives to be expressed without apology as Black and Italian, questioning a public culture used to seeing white as the colour of national heritage. They expose the hypocrisy of Europeans leading hybrid lives but expecting something else from migrants, as illustrated by Heather Merrill's (2015) study of Turin neighbourhoods thick with kebab shops, mosques, African hairstylists, Chinese grocers and Senegalese restaurants, enabling 'non-Western ways of perceiving, being, and knowing [to] interweave with Italian perceptions, ontologies, and knowledges' (p. 81), while migrants 'struggle against routine degradation, vulnerability, and denial of their personhood' (p. 83), and women of African descent are unable to 'walk into a piazza or take public transportation . . . without the risk of being given what Frantz Fanon referred to as "the look", stared at, or harassed' (p. 84). On such ground we see how markers of national belonging stigmatize migrant citizens, as illustrated by Jean Beaman's (2017) Parisian ethnography of university-educated second-generation North Africans defining themselves as French, but feeling othered by a mainstream culture defining Frenchness on 'who "looks French"' (p. 13) rather than on 'professional success, educational attainment, or adhering to Republican ideology' (p. 14).

The grain of lived experience reveals evolving and mixed identities. As Viola Raheb (2017) observes, presumptions of

> cultural and/or religious background . . . as an indicator that [refugees] will not be able to belong, or that their 'difference' will at the very least be a stumbling block . . . are based on a static definition of identity. They overlook the fact that the development of identity is an ongoing process that is driven by

meeting and interacting with others as well as by reflecting on who you are. (p. 131)

Raheb cites the intricacies of her own identity: 'I hold Austrian citizenship, my cultural background is Arabic, or to be more specific, Middle Eastern, my ethnic roots are Palestinian and I was born the daughter of a Christian Palestinian family. The question of my identity or belonging – or anyone else's for that matter – is thus from the beginning very complex, multidimensional, dynamic and as such ever changing' (Raheb, 2017: 131). This is the dynamic of the urban life of natives and settlers alike, defying essentialist definitions of self, race, religion, community and nation so comprehensively picked apart by Anthony Appiah (2018). It proposes belonging as anything but fixed and identity as a poor marker of the shared turf, prompting observers of mixed neighbourhoods and conflict zones such as Jeremy MacClancy (2016) to conclude that in focusing on 'bids to proclaim or manipulate identity, we run the real risk of forgetting that, given the evidence, most people are not much interested in identity. Indeed, the very opposite: they strive daily to uphold equality, commonality and a notion of humanity which usually tends towards the universal. They wish to connect, not divide' (p. 23).

Perhaps MacClancy plays down the degree of urban division and conflict, but the significance of his claim lies in the proposition that meanings of belonging – local and national – could be derived from practices of living together rather than fictions of cultural heritage and true identity that de facto privilege some people over others, demand cultural assimilation as a condition of belonging and reduce heterogenous lives to fixed identity positions (Chin, 2017; Modood, 2018). In freeing public understanding of belonging from suffocating identity markers, new possibilities are opened, including 'the co-ownership principle of belonging ... that, in a world of difference, no core identity is excluded in the running of society and none is subordinate. Home is inclusion. Home is where the "other" is' (Klug, 2017: 123). Belonging, for Brian Klug, is the union of 'diverse pairs of hands jointly on the rudder' (p. 129), where the 'question is not only about bridging differences of culture, it is also about overcoming the disparity in status written into the script of colonial history, whether that history is remembered the way Europe imagines it ("the White Man's burden") or the way non-Europeans experienced it' (p. 128). Belonging conceived as union presumes meaningful co-ownership premised on reparative justice and sensitivity to subaltern social experience. As Joao Biehl and Peter Locke (2010) argue from their ethnographies of conflict in Brazil and Bosnia, those who suffer

> bear an understanding of their worlds, of the social problems they must circumvent or transcend, and of the kind of politics that would actually serve their aspirations that is unaccounted for in policy discussions and decisions. This is not a subjugated knowledge, constituted unidirectionally by power, but something personal, bearing traces of singularity not easily framed or contained. Even when institutionally ignored, it persists, and could be better attended to in the public sphere. (p. 336)

The above examples of everyday negotiations of difference (admittedly in Europe's cities, but still caught in the firestorms of nativist nationalism) gesture meanings of belonging based on co-occupancy and encounter, evocative of Roberto Esposito's (2022) metaphor 'improper community' signalling joint effort and Jean-Luc Nancy's (2000) oxymoron 'singular plural' indicating the union of the individual and common. These are not terms that will fire the public imagination in the way that the chimes of nativist nation do, but they lay out an important alternative of belonging for progressives to work with. For Robert Young (2016), this is the 'possibility of community constructed on the idea of ... individuals who remain singular individuals but in a relation to a community which has no boundaries or lines of exclusion' (p. 18). Young asks 'what relation such singularities may have to each other in a philosophical context in which totalities and essences, and the politics of identity formation founded on sameness and an excluded other, have been disallowed.... How do you theorize a community without closure, without othering, a community which allows the singularity and difference of each of its members?' (p. 18). One political response might be to present nation and belonging as the encounter integral to community, democratically negotiated for reciprocal benefit: community as a contact zone with particular rules of engagement, in its own right the territory of belonging (Sternfeld, 2017). Thomas Claviez (2016), echoing Judith Butler's claim that people everywhere today live in conditions of unwilled adjacency, proposes 'thinking about community as metonymic', in the sense that 'we share nothing but the sheer space of the earth's surface ... in which we are contiguous and contingent upon each other; we do not, as traditional, metaphoric conceptualizations suggest, share a third that implies either a transcendent abstraction, an essence, or a dynastic and patriarchic genealogy' (p. 46). An understanding of community as the challenge of social contiguity and copresence requires working with rather than erasing the anomalous and different, for example, through conciliations of dialogue and democratic procedure, expansions of the commons (Amin and Howell, 2016), collaborations of coproduced 'things, people and spaces' (Wetzel, 2016: 171), and the collective provisions of shared infrastructures, services and institutions.

These redefinitions imagine community as relationally constituted. In her wide-ranging intellectual history of the term 'relation' that looks across the Scottish enlightenment and non-Western ideas of kinship with nature, Marilyn Strathern (2020) challenges its common meaning as the encounter between separate entities with already given identities. In this commonplace, 'parties in "we-relationships" think of themselves as sharing a community of time, a simultaneity of consciousness, each in the spatial proximity of companion others', coalescing around 'the similarities contained in the relations they recognize, where the intentions of strangers are suspect and where outsiders who cannot be ignored must be either assimilated or absolutely kept at bay' (p. 176). Strathern traces a counter-history of affiliation in which 'relation to the other precedes identity; relation secures the difference of things; relation to the self can escape the dialectics of self and other' (p. 88), all three sustaining a public culture accepting the 'interrelatedness and interdependence of phenomena' (p. 167). She recovers a rich legacy of societal understanding of belonging as being-in-relation with others, to extract a vocabulary of 'anonymous civility' (p. 177), 'positive companionship' (p. 182) and 'associational solidarity' (p. 178), recognizing the swarms of interaction (Carter, 2013) and practices of social commonality and public familiarity (Blokland and Nast, 2014; Duyvendak and Wekker, 2016) that characterize lived experience.

This vocabulary unsettles identity conventions premised on separateness. It strengthens reparative work to dismantle ingrained lines of distinction with searing consequences. Paul Gilroy (2016) argues, for example, that 'the damage done by racism, raciology, racialism, and racial hierarchy requires particular forms of acknowledgment. They must involve not only political and juridical gestures but also philosophical ones. They must amount to significantly more than a vague admission that people are doomed always to do bad, hurtful things to each other' (p. 118). They require, for Gilroy, an 'antiracist and reparative humanism . . . warranted by its detailed, critical grasp of the damage done to ethics, truth, and democracy by racial discourses that would not be undone even by the therapeutic grotesqueries of "identity politics" that Fanon swiftly dismissed elsewhere as "the Fraud of a black world"' (p. 122). A vocabulary of the relation that begins to accept that the 'inconvenience of other people' is constitutive of social relations as Laurent Berlant (2022) argues, could 'become a resource for building solidarity and alliance across ambivalence, rather than appearing mainly as the negative sandpaper of sociality' (p. 8) because of sovereign fantasies of us versus them.

A shift in focus from identity to relation includes seeing the nation as a space of malleable and stretched borders, and community as a constellation of interacting subjects near and afar. In Europe, where nativism rings of colonial pretensions, a progressive relational politics has to rectify why 'the history of violence to Europe's "others" perceived as external – primarily colonial violence – remains insufficiently acknowledged in public discourses and divorced from analyses of contemporary violence to non-European migrant populations' (Kovačević, 2018: 119). Its public campaigns must ask: 'What did we do to their countries in the past? What are we doing to them now? What does that have to do with who they are, who we are, and why they are here?' (Mufti, 2007: 19). Its answers must acknowledge the global interdependencies and reciprocities from which national belonging has arisen 'in movement, in melancholy nomadism', through anything but 'fixed identity markers' (Kovačević, 2018: 157). There are many resources at hand. One is Elizabeth Buettner's (2016) account of how colonial legacies have shaped every aspect of the meaning of the UK, France, the Netherlands and Portugal since the mid-twentieth century. There are global cartographies of the European Union, generally assumed to be nation states contained by the Mediterranean and therefore closed to countries to the East and South, despite the Union's incorporation of territory in colonial Africa and Asia at its inception. Peo Hansen and Stefan Jonsson (2014, 2017) reveal how 'the process of European integration was intimately tied to colonialism, so much so, in fact, that the EU's founders in the 1950s made a point of stressing its massive extra-European scope, which was then designated as Eurafrica and institutionalized and codified in the Rome Treaty's colonial association regime that incorporated all of the member states' colonial possessions, most of all in Africa' (2017: 3). In 1957, with France and Belgium still possessing overseas territories, more than three-fourths of the EEC's land area lay outside continental Europe, intended to make the new Europe 'sustainable and prosperous thanks to its incorporation of Africa', and 'strengthened by the shared goal of African development' (p. 6). For the architects of the new European Community, Eurafrica 'was the mediating institutional formation through which Africa and Europe exited the colonial era and entered a new world order where ... their unequal relationship essentially remained unchanged' (p. 27). To know better of Africa as part of 'Europe' would be to rethink contemporary European hostility to migration as well as to acknowledge reparative responsibilities.

As Astrid Van Weyenberg argues, 'from a postcolonial and global perspective, Europeanness can no longer be about possessing a pre-defined cultural identity or about sharing a past. ... The focus has to be on imagining and actively constructing a shared future in which all citizens of Europe are placed *within* a "Europe" that is forever changing' (2019: 66). A first step would be to acknowledge – in educational curricula and in public culture – that national identities in Europe have no meaning outside of past and ongoing global relations. Then the presumptions of native nation would begin to seem anomalous. As Marion Demossier observes for one polity,

> French republicanism and the values it encapsulates is the framework through which belonging is framed .... Claiming that you do not feel French is an insult to Frenchness and the same applies to a lesser extent to being a republican. Most of the debates which have surrounded Muslims in France have

been constructed in such a fashion that they leave little space for a more creative and modern understanding of what it means to live together. (2017: 63)

To see the nation in Europe and beyond from its multiple historical geographies is to look for other sources of unity, for example, civic solidarity in the public sphere (Habermas, 2012) or a political arena of vigorously interactive democracy (Balibar, 2015).

People's Nation, Civic Nation

The prime political question for a new language of belonging is to match the affective power of nativist rhetoric that preys on popular anxieties of sequestered community. Its challenge is to offer a charismatic account, backed by tangible material reforms, of national journey from bad to better times premised on the common and mutual. Perhaps the empathies among strangers and towards the vulnerable that have grown during the pandemic have made more room for these virtues, as do the demands of the climate emergency requiring concerted collective stewardship and stakeholder cooperation at home and abroad. But these are fickle, quickly turning into sentiments of aversion and isolationism when the emergencies are felt to threaten self-interest, especially when accompanied by a powerful protectionist rhetoric of blame of the sort unleashed by the Trump and Bolsonaro regimes against foreign countries, elites, subjects and ideas for causing the emergencies. Relational ideas of belonging require the mobilization of an imaginary of nation and national attachment able to denaturalize the nativist imaginary. This section discusses ideas of civic nation that might be able to find traction, after scanning the affective dynamics of resurgent nationalism in some new and old democracies.

Alina Polyakova and Neil Fligstein (2016) claim that the surge in nationalism across Europe stems from popular dissatisfaction with the EU since the onset of the world financial crisis in 2007. They find that despite the roots of national economic recession and inequality in the failures of the world banking system and the deliberate choices of some countries to impose harsh austerity measures, the EU has attracted disproportionate blame for its policies of free movement within the EU, its stringent bailout conditions and the power of remote bureaucrats and politicians in Brussels or Strasbourg. They cite a Pew Research Center survey showing that the proportion of citizens across the Union with a positive opinion of the EU declined from 60 to 45 per cent between 2005 and 2013, as well as Eurobarometer surveys demonstrating that citizens declaring exclusively national identities rose from 41 to 46 per cent in the period 2005–10, while those declaring national and European identities dropped from 48 to 41 per cent. For Polyakova and Fligstein, this change stems from public perception 'that enforcing austerity policies in the face of economic downturn was more important to European political authorities than the well-being of citizens in any given country', pushing publics in member states to 'look to the nation and not Europe for solutions and decreased a sense of European solidarity' (p. 65). Importantly, however, negative public perception of the EU is not divorced from explicit mobilization by nationalist forces in the media and political arena against European membership as the source of national misery. Europe has been made 'the vanishing point of the radical right's program and of the growing popular revolt against the tired post-war liberal consensus' (Kallis, 2018: 68), its liberalism, open borders, remote and unaccountable bureaucracy and welfare stringencies cited as the source of national economic, political and cultural crisis.

In the newer European democracies such as Poland and Hungary, their has been a backlash against an EU perceived to be slave to (neo)liberal values and to the more powerful Western economies, with far right power also drawing on sharp internal divisions over post-communist national identity precipitated by persistent economic malaise. Clara Hendrickson (2018) explains that in Poland and Hungary nativist aversion to the open society is tied to these divisions: 'about four in ten citizens hold negative views of growing diversity, and majorities believe their society is better off when composed of people from the same nationality, religion, and culture' (p. 47). Questions of national identity and cultural preservation have risen to the centre of political discourse, to become the conduit of anxieties of economic and social displacement. Through incessant vilification of progressives, the judiciary and liberal institutions, the political far right and its sponsored civic associations have peddled myths of national greatness freed from imperial, communist and liberal shackles, entrusted to a strong nationalist state to restore a lost historical prosperity and pride. Hendrickson writes,

> Today, Kaczynski and Orban do not merely promise to enshrine an ethnocentric conception of national identity into public life and laws; they also frame illiberalism as a pragmatic path toward economic prosperity. Orban, laying out his vision for an illiberal democracy, stated, 'We are searching for and we are doing our best to find – parting ways with Western European dogmas, making ourselves independent from them – the form of organizing a community, that is capable of making us competitive in this great world-race'. (p. 53)

In power, the Orbán and Kaczynski governments have perfected a narrative of the healthy, tradition-bound society protected by the strong state shielding itself from the sickness of a liberal democracy that has made the rest of Europe 'a decadent land with no future' (Krastev, 2020: 72). They have sought public approval in redefining citizenship as a blood right in the ethnic nation freed from the long shadow of Ottoman, Hapsburg, Soviet, EU, corporate and liberal rule. Populist resentment in Europe's older democracies has also turned to cultural heritage to find traction. As Sertan Akbaba (2018) observes, 'the populist parties across Europe represent themselves as the defenders of European values, culture, and ... more broadly a European civilization with the motto of "Europe for Europeans"' (p. 205). They do so in the name of the ordinary citizen seeing through the obfuscations of elite liberal politics, with 'words like "protection", "secure", "fight", "cope", "overcome", which are all carefully picked' (p. 211) to place a body-politics of hatred at the centre of their endeavour. The parallels of cultural body-politics are striking, shown in Hendrickson's (2018) comparison of how the French National Front (relabelled National Rally) names the same enemies as the Hungarian and Polish far right, decrying 'Islam as an attack on French identity, globalism as an attack on French economic prosperity and its social model, and the political establishment an attack on French democracy' (p. 55). Like the far right elsewhere, it links popular misery and alienation to a liberal political establishment selling out to transnational capital, European rules and multiculturalism, and it promises a return to wellbeing and security by cleansing France of migration, cultural dilution and Islam, restoring popular democracy, and a campaign to 'reindustrialize France, nationalize commercial banks, and increase the generosity of the French social safety net' (p. 57). Similarly, the Italian far right – weaving in and out of government – rails against a 'corrupt' national and EU political establishment, cultural dilution by migrants and cosmopolitans, economic and welfare policy biases against the white working class, and a liberalism sacrificing homeland traditions and the protected national economy. In Brexit Britain, the Conservative government has pursued the same politics of nationalist sovereignty by differentiating deserving 'left-behind' 'somewheres' from usurping 'nowheres', railing against the

European Union, parliamentary procedure, the civil service, the judiciary and the liberal media, and harbouring old colonial ambitions while giving free reign to xenophobia, racism and Islamophobia. The tactics of the Trump administration and the Republican Party, now regrouping for office, has been no different, its campaign to make America great again knowing no limits in kicking democratic procedure, fabricating lies, subverting the law, and mobilizing the shock troops to make way for the ethno-cultural nation. In Brazil, the Bolsonaro government deployed the same rhetoric and violence to inflame an expectant population told stories of betrayal by preceding Workers' Party (PT) administrations and urban elites.

The rallies of native nation have become the passing point of political battle in the strained democracies, their opponents having to reckon with the appeal of authoritarian populism while derailed by its violent tactics. In Europe, for example, opposition in the arc of countries from Greece, Spain and Portugal through France, the Benelux countries and Germany to the Scandinavian states in the throes of a tussle between (neo) liberal cosmopolitanism, nativist nationalism and Left critique of austerity and unbridled capitalism, shares a nervousness to openly confront far-right xenophobic and ethno-culturalist discourse. Progressive cause for better national protections for the left-behind while committing to internationalism and multiculturalism has tended to befuddle electorates, overshadowed by an emotive identity politics tapping into historical anxieties of invasive people, creeds and cultures. Discussions of national identity, sovereign subjects and authentic traditions have become obligatory to public debate, all parties obliged to declare on who belongs, which values and customs should prevail, and how domestic interests are best protected, across the spectrum of concerns over national economic prosperity, social equality and political autonomy. Thus, though nationalist support in this arc of countries waxes and wanes between electoral cycles, the more decisive achievement of nativists has been to alter the meaning and freight of national identity and sovereignty.

This may help to explain, for example, the 'pessimistic turn' in the Netherlands across the political spectrum, uneasy about an earlier period of colonial guilt favouring multiculturalism, pluralism and internationalism. Forces on the right and left claiming to speak for the silent majority are seeking restrictions on asylum and migration and invoking old models of assimilationist integration of foreigners. They feel free to accuse Dutch Muslims of harbouring anti-Western and seditious ambitions and to express regret over the loss of a communitarian way of life, regardless of the evidence (Lucassen and Lucassen, 2015). Similarly, further north, the nativist Sweden Democrats with unexpected ease have forced discussion of 'Swedishness' into the idea of Sweden as the 'people's home' (*folkhem*) honed by the Social Democrats over the twentieth century to mean the home of social equality and inclusion based on the managed economy, liberal freedoms and the strong welfare state. The Sweden Democrats have upturned the settled meaning of this idea, which required natives and settlers 'following or surrendering to the system: trusting the government, working and paying taxes, and respecting the rights of others to be individuals in a society that champions rights of women, children, LGBTQ people, and people with disabilities' (Miller, 2017: 389). For them, now close to the reins of power, the people's home has been destroyed by neoliberalism and elite politics and by divisions sowed by migration and multiculturalism, necessitating border controls, the strong and interventionist state, selective welfare and old values and customs to return the equal and cohesive society (Airas and Truedsson, 2023). The Sweden Democrats have managed to give the *folkhem* a much darker meaning, putting migrants, minorities and cosmopolitans on test on grounds of cultural conformity (Pettersson et al., 2016).

Nativist populism succeeded in proposing ethno-nationalist sovereignty as the solution to public disillusionment with liberal democracy, welfare austerity and internationalism. For Partha Chatterjee (2019), the

> most palpable symptom of the crisis is the collapse, in one country after another, of the credibility of traditional political parties and leaders whose organizational resources and moral legitimacy served as the pillars on which bourgeois hegemony had rested for at least the last half a century, if not longer. Those representatives – the hitherto benign and often revered public faces of class power – are now being targeted by populist campaigners as a political class that has sold out to the moneybags and entrenched itself in every institution of power. (p. 117)

Out of unrelenting talk of grass-roots sacrifice met by ethnonationalist pride and policies, has arisen 'a sudden burst of popular energy around leaders and movements asserting the moral claims of the people-nation' (p. 71). Symptomatic is the surge to power of the Hindu nationalists led by Modi in India over the last decade, whose pastiche of the deserving poor, Hindu sublime, Muslim encroachment, liberal decadence, corrupt political and economic establishment, deep pre-colonial history and failed secular democracy has earned it vast popular support, around the promise of a free and prosperous future for the masses in a proud and powerful Hindu nation (Dasgupta, 2019; Bhargava, 2023). Public opposition to this reworking of the meaning of India, and to the violence it has heaped on the many who have been declared unwanted or enemies, has been vocal, principled and persistent, but the swift institutional takeovers and constitutional assaults of the Bharatiya Janata Party (BJP), together with the mobilization of its vast capillary networks and demotic politics in and out of parliament has denuded Congress and other anti-nationalist parties, along with India's post-independence political imaginary, of the inclusive secular society.

The accommodations of place discussed earlier, and explored in more detail in the next chapter, remain by definition situated negotiations of difference, on their own no substitute for a cultural politics of nation able to confront nativist nationalism with another narrative of belonging. What could this narrative look like? It has become difficult for progressives to defend prevalent ideas of nation rooted in universal welfare, the rule of law, liberal democracy, social solidarity and cultural pluralism, with these precepts linked by nationalists to native inequality and exclusion, and with public culture obsessing homeland subjects, sovereignty and tradition. Liberal and social democratic forces have chosen silence or adopted a language of border controls and welfare selectivity, while turning to policies to take the sting out of the politics of resentment (e.g. by improving access to work, welfare and services). They have also begun to court a language of patriotism appealing to a shared way of life and traditions such as tolerance, fairness or hospitality so as to win back disillusioned majorities while reassuring minorities and cosmopolitans. In Europe especially, another homeland narrative to neutralize nativism is emerging, appealing to softer forms of patriotism such as 'trust between neighbors that comes from a shared attachment to territory and the language and customs that prevail there' (Scruton, 2019: 42) or 'devotion to a particular place and a particular way of life, which one believes to be the best in the world but has no wish to force on other people', as George Orwell ([1945] 2018: 2) proposed at the end of the Second World War to distinguish patriotism from nationalism.

Other propositions settle on certain moral precepts. Steven B. Smith (2019: 597) suggests a civic patriotism to confront Trumpian nativism that kindles popular interest in the 'highest, most universal moral principles' without 'fantasies of blood and soil' enshrined in the country's founding documents. For Smith, American patriotism at its origins 'is a patriotism of ideas. In this crucial respect, the United States is . . . a nation founded upon the principles of modern philosophy. Our founding document, the Declaration of Independence, is dedicated to the proposition that all men are created equal' (p. 597). This Americanness, for Smith, celebrates 'civility, law-abidingness, respect for others, responsibility, love of honor, courage, and loyalty' (p. 603), virtues of 'pride, service, and loyalty that bind together members of a nation and make them citizens' (p. 598). Moral patriotism, for Francis Fukuyama (2018) gets past the biases of customary nationalism by identifying a general will and a generic people, rather than specific individuals. Fukuyama writes the

> U.S. Constitution begins with the statement: 'We the People of the United States, in Order to form a more perfect Union, establish Justice, insure domestic Tranquility, provide for the common Defence, promote the general Welfare, and secure the Blessings of Liberty to ourselves and our Posterity, do ordain and establish this Constitution for the United States of America'. The Constitution says clearly that the people are sovereign and that legitimate government flows from their will. But it does not define who the people are, or the basis on which individuals are to be considered part of the national community'. (pp. 12–13)

Fukuyama warns that without strong sentiments of civic patriotism, 'democracies will not survive if citizens are not in some measure irrationally attached to the ideas of constitutional government and human equality through feelings of pride and patriotism. These attachments will see societies through their low points, when institutions are failing to deliver and reason alone may counsel despair' (p. 11).

The customary patriotism of Scruton and Orwell tends not to stray far from the nationalist choice to focus on cultural traditions, but the civic patriotism of Smith and Fukuyama, turning to universal moral principles, clears new ground for a progressive politics of belonging. But its work is cut out in democracies lacking the constitutional or political enshrinement of these principles from which popular affinity can grow, and whose histories of imagined community have long relied on demarcations of territory, ethnicity, class, faith and tradition to define the nation. In most of the democracies discussed above, the purchase of moral patriotism falters beyond the commemorative occasion, under pressure from other ingrained traditions of national unity mobilized by nationalists to even mock it as the ruling ploy of rootless cosmopolitan elites. In turn, the history of constitutional universalism, where it does exist, is not innocent in its selections of the humans who count as bearers or beneficiaries of the binding virtues. The universal ideals of the American Declaration of Independence and the US Constitution were forged on a legacy of slavery that wrote the Black population out of membership of the 'sovereign people' by considering its members less than human or 'American'. They have looked on silently or complicitly during the long history of racism against the country's African American, indigenous and migrant populations formally counted as citizens but treated as inferiors and strangers in most other ways. In America and elsewhere, the civic patriotism of founding virtues rests on colour-coded understandings of the sovereign people, it too acquiescent or silenced by nationalist identity politics.

A more prosaic but surer virtuous politics of civic nation could simply commit to the principle of the just society, based on advocacy for generalized capability and wellbeing, deepened and expanded democracy, socio-economic and spatial equality, and recompense for harms of injustice, exclusion and discrimination. These are not fanciful slogans of a tired egalitarian politics measuring nation by the strength of its provisions and protections, but they capture the quest for universal care, fellowship and security that arises in the face of perpetual emergency (from Covid-19 to the climate crisis) as well as intersectional distaste for gender, sexual and racial violence, as exemplified by the #MeToo and Black Lives Matter movements. There is interest across society for the protective state, the fair economy and society and the secure existential environment, with inclusivity and mutuality firmly in the frame. At least for now. There are strong signs of demand for the just society in the public culture of troubled democracies, especially among younger generations, women and urban dwellers dismayed by the egocentricities and exclusions of nativist nationalism. By unambiguously rejecting austerity, precarity, welfare parsimony and unregulated capitalism – whose combined effect has been to ravage the lives of the least well off in the most vulnerable places – progressive parties could dare to take a principled stance against racism, xenophobia and illiberalism in the name of the common good in a just society. They could promise a programme of investment in health and welfare equity, job and income security, fair access to housing and education, accountable and participatory government, decisive action against hate and discrimination, stringent rules of institutional, market and corporate behaviour, and preparations against environmental hazard and risk. The list for such a politics of the just society is endless at a time of corrosion of everything equal, stable and safe. Its challenge remains that of framing the possibilities as a narrative of belonging, one that confronts the nationalist imaginary but also looks beyond the state 'guaranteeing rights' or 'supporting a particular vision of the good life' (O'Brien, 2016: 30).

What could this involve? One option is to frame the quests of the just society as those of the nation that commits to 'the common good above the pursuit of any individual or factional ends' (Skinner, 1990: 304). This simple step signals more than the liberal premise that historically 'freedom and social solidarity have been able to coexist' (Chin, 2017: 296), each acting 'as a check on the excesses of the other' (p. 303). The return of nationalism has exposed the fallacies of this assumption and requires more explicit progressive advocacy for the nation of the common good, nudged by public rehearsal of principles such as human solidarity (Bhargava, 2023) and non-racial humanism (Gilroy, 2016) as the measures of belonging. This step must attend to the practice itself of democracy, according to Pankaj Mishra 'in such disfavour in so many countries around the world because most people see it as something that has no substance whatsoever, that is simply providing cover to the beneficiaries of the system' (Taylor and Mishra, 2019: 28). Mishra asks for 'institutions that are responsive, that are actually sensitive to the simple idea that democracy is literally the rule of the people . . . . decentralisation and centring citizens' (p. 27). In turn, a politics of the just society could seek to disarm populist critique of elite liberal democracy by standing by a genuinely participatory public and political sphere that trusts the outcomes of distributed responsibility and democratic dialogue among and between citizens and accountable institutions (see chapter 3).

The challenge for a progressive politics is to add substance to an understanding of nation as 'composite community in relation' as Édouard Glissant (1997) proposed for a post-colonial Caribbean carried by the interactions of a freed plural citizenry. It could make more of extant relations in shared spaces: the commonalities of the classroom, playing field, workplace and interest group; the experiments of sharing in the circular and social economy and in communal forms of living; the diplomacies of engagement in public space and in inclusive sites of the public sphere; the struggles united against environmental destruction, poverty and inequality, and conflict and violence. From this territory, the nation could be projected as the composite of overlapping interests and shared practices and spaces (Amin and Howell, 2016), no longer an imagined community of particular values, traditions and peoples, but a space of conciliations. In this way, the politics of belonging, constrained by nativism's rewriting of the nation as a war of identities, and liberalism's practice of uneven individual freedoms, could attend to the quality of common and associational life and to intersectional discriminations that work against some communities. More broadly, it could establish new forms of political assembly harnessing humans and nonhumans from diverse geographies to an object-oriented struggle to ensure the survival of all (Latour and Weibel, 2005; Morton, 2013). In doing so, it could help citizens look past the nation as a territorial body of sovereign subjects and ethno-cultural pasts, towards a 'terrestrial' politics involving getting 'down to earth' with all kinds of allies in all kinds of places in pursuit of a safer and nourishing dwelling environment (Latour, 2018). This terrestrial politics of the common could dare to dissent with nation-centred wisdom on the body politic and its constituencies by attending to the life-giving layers of the earth's ground and atmosphere now at risk (Latour et al., 2020) and by mobilizing hybrid kinships and rhizomatic connections to tackle the problems of coexistence (Haraway, 2016; Fuller and Goriunova, 2019).

In sum, the response to nativist nationalism does not have to dwell on liberal freedoms or the legacy of custom, identity and tradition to advance its cause, always troubled by the elusive line between the liberal or cultural inside and outside in the thoroughly plural and mixed societies most democracies have become. There are other ideas of civic nation, democratic convention and common cause that can be mobilized to convince publics as necessary for individual and collective survival. We should leave behind the introspective tradition of seeing nation as a set of moral and cultural distinctions, typified by David Hume in the mid-eighteenth century in his observation:

> We may often remark a wonderful mixture of manners and characters in the same nation, speaking the same language, and subject to the same government... Where the government of

a nation is altogether republican, it is apt to beget a peculiar set of manners. Where it is altogether monarchical it is more apt to have the same effect; the imitation of superiors spreading the national manners faster among the people. If the governing part of state consist altogether of merchants, as in Holland, their uniform way of life will fix their character. . . . The genius of a particular sect or religion is also apt to mould the manner of a people. (cited in Jensen, 2016: 9)

The resurgent wars waged in the name of national manners – secular, religious, republican, mercantile – can be avoided.

Conclusion

There are many options for a progressive politics of belonging to confront nativism. They lie in rehearsing nation not as cultural or historical fact but as a zone of engagement where the terms of hospitality, worldliness and common endeavour matter for the wellbeing of citizens, old and new, extant and expectant, irrespective of the distributions of welfare. In exposing the follies and fallacies of nativism, the progressive cause must endeavour to alter both the lives of the left-behind and the affective language of imagined community, recognizing their separate but connected agency. Liberal and social democratic parties would be wrong to think that policies to reduce social division, inequality and disadvantage will win over the discontented. They cannot pretend that insecure majorities attracted to an imaginary of the enclave nation of old settlers and customs can be won back without being offered another reassuring counter-imaginary of belonging that shifts public perception of what the nation is and who it is for, what makes for strength and unity. The ideas of civic nation proposed here may lack the immediate appeal (or distastefulness) of blood and soil cajolements of community, but this is reason for progressives to build a politics of affect around them (e.g. through the arts outlined in chapter 3) instead of just hoping for better times.

Rebecca Bryant and Daniel Knight (2019) argue that popular trust in a politics of the future is guided by how it manages anticipation, expectation, hope, potentiality and destiny. Nativism has worked these senses through shock and awe tactics making way for a homely life beyond the turbulent present, tilting popular hope and expectation towards a nationalist future perceived as destined and just. The challenge for progressive politics is to find a way of harnessing these senses to a futurity of collective and communal engagement with the different, unknown and hazardous no longer denied but faced as the field of anticipation and expectation but also hope and potentiality. This could involve, as Les Back (2021) writes, recovering a spirit of 'worldly hope' to denude hollow utopias, citing everyday moments of conviviality and joint custodianship, refusing to give way in the face of hate and division. It could involve, as this chapter has also argued, effort to kindle public expectation and desire around the open and plural civic nation. Differently from nativist firestorms, the community to come could be portrayed as the utopia that 'is never no-where, an imagined perfected future, but always already potentially exists in the now-here, in our collective fidelity to the project of making a world we so desire rather than a world we fear' (Wegner, 2020: 218). There was such a sense of the future in the moments after mid-twentieth century fascism and Nazism and it can be rekindled by looking up from existing practices of cohabitation and common endeavour.

2
Street Affinities

Introduction

The preceding chapter cited examples of shared coexistence in Europe's cities with little resemblance to nativist discourse of cultural and ethnic incompatibility, though not immune from its claims of poor indigenous lives robbed by encroaching migrants and minorities. They highlighted the gap between life practices and purist imaginaries of nation. In focusing on social interactions and shared aspirations, the examples only gestured at the sutures of place, which are more explicitly explored in this chapter through an analysis of biographies of wellbeing and attachment in a Delhi slum and homeless strip. In Southern democracies like India gripped by nationalist fervour, political animosities often focus on the neglect of a vast 'native' population crammed in dilapidated slums, informal settlements and urban peripheries. It is presumed that in this expansive territory of scarcity, precarity and hardship, feelings of resentment prevail among settlers awaiting fulfilment of their citizenship rights. This population is often politically invoked or mobilized in communalist riots against elites, minorities, authorities and religious others, called out onto the street or goaded into attacking tarnished neighbours. Yet, past the moments of escalation, relations between people from diverse backgrounds living cheek by jowl in want and hardship remain cordial and peaceful, the infractions of imagined community forgotten or refracted through senses of belonging formed in shared place attachments. Rhythms of local familiarity and commonality mediate personal biographies and interpersonal relations through the tie of the coproduced habitat, life played out in public and the shared challenge of survival. Contiguous coexistence in these spaces of extreme hardship and infrastructural absence, precariously balanced between alienation and attachment, provide clues for a progressive politics of belonging.

The dynamics of cohabitation observed in this chapter typify life in India's poorest urban settlements at a time of virulent Hindu nationalism promoted by the Modi government and its tentacles across the religious, civic and administrative landscape that have torn into the country's official commitment since independence to state secularism, religious pluralism and constitutional democracy. Backed by massive electoral victories in the last ten years, but building on decades of Hindutva agitation in poor neighbourhoods and religious communities, the promise of this biopolitics has been to give India back to its allegedly neglected Hindu population, precolonial sacred traditions and communalist energies by suppressing constitutional law and democracy, liberal secularism and cosmopolitanism, and rational and scientific knowledge. Through its strong coalition of state, religious, corporate and popular power, Hindutva nationalism has spread with terrifying speed and violence against professionals, liberals, socialists and secular elites, but above all, against Muslims and Islam, by making its politics of cleansing pivotal to a narrative of national freedom and prosperity, in a long tradition of nationalist thought in India premising sovereignty on fratricidal violence (Kapila, 2021). Urban slums and informal settlements have been the breeding ground of the movement, seeking to feed off frustrations of poverty and deprivation that, however, are accompanied by dispositions of cohabitation that survive the agitations producing nationalist votes and riots. The evidence in this chapter speaks to practices of 'worldly hope' formed in practices of joint survival in places where spatial affordances have replaced infrastructural ones in their absence. The evidence does not in any way justify institutional neglect – quite the opposite – but suggests relational orientations of place that might help an India's politics of imagined community still rooted in non-violence, constitutional democracy and the inclusive secular state (assuming it can prove able to improve the lives of the many so long eluded by it).

The iterations of space, subjectivity and belonging explored in this chapter draw on fieldwork in early 2020 in Kusumpur Pahari, an unauthorized colony in South Delhi located near Jawaharlal Nehru University (JNU), and in Yamuna Pushta, a clearing along the river in Old Delhi where the homeless live in makeshift tents or temporary shelters run by an NGO. The contrast between the two settlements could not be more striking. Yamuna Pushta is a narrow strip of land, with official shelters, toilet blocks and food vans located along a busy walkway on the upper level, and informal tents made of wood, plastic and cloth that house individuals, two cinemas and a shop and tea stall, scattered along the lower level behind a large exposed water pipe and amidst trees leading down to the bank of the river Yamuna. Here camp out the poorest, facing abject conditions, wondering about in blankets if not lucky enough to be out for a day's work, huddled around fires, paying a small fee to watch movies, passing the time of day playing cards or Ludo, plying drugs or drink to find some relief from their dire circumstances. The community of single male migrants is physically and mentally stretched, its least able members afflicted by substance addiction, physical impairment or mental disorders, and its most able ones managing to find work for three or four days a month as casual labourers on building sites and at weddings or pushing loaded carts, to stave off hunger and desperation.

Kusumpur Pahari's 40-year history of 'unauthorized' build on land prized for its value still faces the threat of slum demolition to make way for further gentrification in prosperous South Delhi. The colony has grown into a crowded, busy and differentiated poor urban neighbourhood housing some 22,000 people in 1,500 one- or two-roomed dwellings. Its buildings are solid structures of vernacular build and design, serviced by paved but unrepaired roads and alleyways, piped water and electricity, rudimentary drains, trucks of potable water arriving every few days, street sweepers and waste-disposal trucks, and communal toilet blocks. Most of these services, including free water and electricity and food rations for the majority of its low-income households, have arrived only in recent years thanks to the pro-poor interventions of the municipal administration, greatly alleviating the burden and cost of existence in the settlement. Made up of dark alleyways of cramped dwellings, the main streets are lined with small shops and enterprises, clearings and public spaces, places of worship, clinics and food stalls. They gather a heavy traffic of motorbikes, bicycles, humans, animals and private life spilling over from the dwellings. In the settlement all manner of difference and diversity are closely juxtaposed. In one opening next to a municipal dump attracting scavenging animals, children might play near a parking lot where men get intoxicated, sharing the space with older residents sitting on plastic chairs. At the edge of the settlement on rubbish-strewn open ground where pigs, cows, children, commuters and drinkers rub along, mothers might collect borehole water next to a group of destitute women huddled around a fire outside a noisy elementary school.

This diversity is mirrored in the social composition of the settlement. Its families belong to diverse castes and religions from various north Indian regions. Apart from a minority of early settlers who have done well in business or professionally, most families are poor and earn around 20,000 Rupees (£200) a month. But this poverty is differentiated. The older families tend to have better houses, with husbands, wives and adult children working as white-collar workers, artisans, drivers, rickshaws owners, caretakers, cleaners and shop assistants in South Delhi's many thriving commercial and public ventures or middle-class homes, or in other localities connected by Vasant Vihari metro station, a stone's throw from the settlement. More recent arrivals, and less fortunate or stigmatized families such as Muslims and Dalits, tend to live in poorer accommodation, finding work in low-paid, unskilled and casual jobs, or remaining outside the labour market and in secondary education or professional training. There are also strong gender and generational differences, exemplified by women and girls from more traditional families held back in work and education by patriarchal constraints, and by many young men drawn to alcohol and drugs from a very early age, eventually becoming unemployed and physically and mentally ill. This variety makes it difficult to generalize about people and place in Kusumpur Pahari, one reason why the discussion below unfolds through particular biographies of belonging.

The biographies are drawn from conversations with residents and street observations about how habitat and dwelling fold into affliction and affiliation. Walking the streets and alleyways, stopping in public spaces and visiting places of worship and learning prompted many conversations, offering a glimpse of the lives of men and women of different ages, backgrounds and social status. During cold and foggy January days punctuated every few minutes by the roar of flights about to land at Indira Gandhi International Airport, Gunjesh Kumar and I (sometimes accompanied by Maan Barua) probed into individual biographies, senses of place and social outlooks. Observing people in their surroundings – the state of homes, public spaces, infrastructures, services, streets, spaces of worship, physical atmospheres – helped us understand the reciprocities of place and social experience, sometimes discussed with residents and professionals with long experience of community life in the settlement. The investigation in Yamuna Pushta was shorter and more mediated, conscious of the reticence of the homeless to engage directly and for long. Amid the trees and in nearby housing and medical shelters run by NGOs unfolded brief conversations with the homeless about their circumstances and attachments, enriched by information from professionals working at the shelters. Our key informant and guide was Gufran Alam, a social worker at the Centre for Equity Studies (CES) with oversight for the homeless. CES is an important source of ground research and practical support for the poor in Delhi. With his own history of ending up on the streets when he first arrived in Delhi, Gufran is well known by the homeless and NGOs working in the field, much valued for his ten-year experience of helping the homeless to secure food, clothing and shelter, and identity documents to qualify for financial, food and medical aid. His deep knowledge of the lives of the homeless, their existential challenges and disorders, their daily practices and coping mechanisms, and the care and support they require, became the touchstone of our understanding of the spatial subjectivities of the homeless.

Respectful of the language of the poor themselves in making sense of their circumstances, including the excess of formal and informal knowledge governing their lives (Das, 2022), this chapter works through words of fragility and endurance encountered in Kusumpur Pahari and Yamuna Pushta to explore the relations of dwelling and encounter that mediate wellbeing and belonging. After a discussion of writing on subjectivity and sociality formed in situated embodied practice, the chapter draws on personal states of being named in the field to reflect on how the interactions of biography, sociality and place affect life-chances, social affinities and senses of belonging. The discussion of states of abjection and withdrawal in the bare environment of Yamuna Pushta, with relations stretched by all but the intermediations of NGOs, is preceded by a discussion of variegations of wellbeing and affiliation in the fuller experiences of place in Kusumpur Pahari.

Embodied Affliction, Contiguous Affinity

In her celebrated book *Affliction*, based on years of research in Delhi's low-income neighbourhoods, Veena Das (2015) shows how experiences of mental and physical suffering are folded bodily and discursively 'into the scene of the everyday' (p. 27). Das finds the poor enduring affliction as yet another test of survival, rendered ordinary by the ongoing drama of living played out in the open as private matters spill out into the public in crowded settlements. She also finds that while the poor incorporate physical and mental ailment into their daily lives, it is often with incomprehension, believing that others know better what's going on. Affliction is 'absorbed in the everyday' as ordinary suffering but also 'creates incoherence' (p. 16) resulting in its neglect or referral to respected members of the community, medical practitioners of various stripes and religious mediums. Through rich stories of individuals, histories of illness and disease and surveys of therapeutic practice, the book reveals the close connections of affliction and everyday life, suffering interpreted through entire bodily biographies, the challenges of slum life and distinctive local vocabularies of illbeing and remedy. In the popular neighbourhood Das finds ailments and their consequences named, felt and negotiated in the unfolding of whole lives led in non-sequential and contradictory ways. To grasp affliction close up, she urges a method sensitive to the disjunctive vocabularies of the poor 'crafted out of this lived experience' and avoiding a 'well-organized narrative with clear plot lines and well-recognized social actors' (p. 18). Das asks for the meaningful bricolage of inordinate life to be taken seriously, analytically and politically.

This is the intention in this chapter, joining a genre of work interpreting social behaviour and affiliation from body-space interactions in specific places. In writing on urban slums and informal settlements, one vein highlights the plight of the poor confronted by precarious living conditions, economic and spatial marginalization, violence and stigmatization, restricted rights and entitlements, and inadequate access to basic infrastructures and services. It reveals the damage of poverty and the injustices of economic and political marginalization, and it proposes remedies based on improved housing conditions and access to infrastructures and services, reinforced rights, entitlements and capabilities, and different forms of restorative justice. Its focus falls on the political economy of exclusion and inclusion, and on the redistributions of power – political, legal, economic and social – that would make a difference to the lives and habitats of the poor. Another complementary vein, largely ethnographic in method, looks at the lives of the poor, their rhythms of survival and their affective dispositions through the entanglements of political economy and biopolitics in bodily experience of circumstance and power. Its account of the poor does not fit into the language of incapacitation or resilience in following the textured intricacies of situated life and subjective agency, revealing varying shades of endurance, negotiation of circumstances and personhood formed in place and with others. This vein foregrounds the vernaculars of the urban poor and the reciprocities of material culture, social experience and political economy shaping states of being and attachment – the grammars of the ground on which the balances of wellbeing and belonging pivot (Amin and Lancione, 2022).

In staying close to the choreography of affliction and affiliation in dwelling practices, this vein of inquiry throws into relief unexpected sites of social suture and fracture. Its examples include Filip de Boeck's studies of possibilities and attachments formed around broken roads, cemeteries and unfinished buildings in Kinshasa (De Boeck and Baloji, 2016); Brighupati Singh's (2015) writing on Sufi shrines in rural India that provide respite, hope and sense of place to the mentally ill and their families; Michele Lancione's (2019) portrayal of living communally with heroin addiction in the underground caverns of Bucharest railway station, with shared company, warm pipelines and cavern furnishings playing their part; Teresa Caldeira's (2012) account of how youths without prospects in the peripheries of São Paulo reassemble through reciprocities of music, art and street vernacular; Tatiana Thieme's (2018) study of youth 'hussle' in the slums of Nairobi to make a living and form relations through waste recycling and an alternative language of meaningful labour and belonging; Joao Biehl's (2013) biography of a woman's mental illness managed through diaries, dreams, fragile love and open grounds in a Brazilian asylum; and my own work with Lisa Richaud on how poor migrants from the countryside in Shanghai manage stress and dislocation through a language of forbearance and prosaic rituals of keeping connected, entertained and informed (Amin and Richaud, 2020; Richaud and Amin, 2020). These ethnographies do not underestimate the hardship and alienation suffered by the poor, but find their temporary mitigation in daily rhythms of survival combining self-initiative, familiarities of people and place, and a local vernacular of managed affliction. They reveal how, in spaces of duress and lack, the unhabitable is made habitable (Simone, 2018) through the assembly of material fragments, useful connections and words and practices of endurance (McFarlane, 2021). They unveil an often ignored urban 'surrounds' (Simone, 2022) composed of improvised contiguities of infrastructure, environment and care that turns out to be important for wellbeing.

This is how the discussion of states of being and belonging in Kusumpur Pahari and Yamuna Pushta is approached, exploring the two sites not as a stage on which social relations simply unfold, but as 'ecologies of experience' (Simpson, 2013), in which subjectivity and sociality form in the moment-to-moment reciprocities of body and habitat (Rose and Fitzgerald, 2022). It looks to how in lived space shared with proximate others, 'inner life processes and affective states' (Biehl et al., 2007: 6) form in the interactions of 'human bodies, nonhuman bodies, animate entities, inanimate objects, ambient atmospheres, sounds, discursive formations, social norms' (Simpson, 2013: 193). It finds susceptibilities of survival and affiliation closely tied to 'dynamics of the "environment"' and 'lived experience of urbanicity' (Fitzgerald et al., 2016: 152) producing the 'topography of the everyday sensibilities ... consequential to living through things' (Stewart, 2011: 445). In short, it finds the questions of national intimacy and aversion towards and between strangers posed in this book refracted through local choreographies of dwelling with others in particular surrounds that generate shades of forbearance and susceptibility.

Choreographies of Forbearance

There is no uniformity of response among residents of Kusumpur Pahari to the common deprivations of cramped housing, uncertain tenure, rudimentary services, environmental degradation, absent privacy and extensive poverty. This is because of differences of residential duration, caste, gender and class position, competence, capability and opportunity, ability to access education and welfare care, and individual and family biographies of wellbeing. This variety is reflected in the vocabulary used by residents to describe their circumstances, mental states and sense of place, illustrated in the three states of forbearance discussed below. Delving into terms used by residents to describe their existential states and affective dispositions, the discussion touches on the intricacies of biography, circumstance and habitat involved, before exploring them more explicitly after the section on the choreographies of survival in Yamuna Pushta.

'Majbuti'

On the first evening after entering Kusumpur Pahari on a cold January day, feeling anxious about who would engage with us and our interest in states of mind over the coming days, we met a man looking for some of his pigs that had strayed down a gulley near his home. To our relief, 'Satish' spoke to us freely and warmly, inviting us to sit around a fire outside his house, drink tea and chat also with his wife. Satish spoke of arriving in the settlement in 2003, working as a caretaker and a cleaner at JNU, bringing up five young children in their tiny well-kept home, keeping pigs to maintain a Dalit rural tradition and to 'stay out of trouble', ensuring the wellbeing of their children and keeping afloat amidst hardship. The couple acknowledged the difficulties of living in the slum: its cramped and under-serviced housing, the constant threat of eviction, the ease with which the young can fall into bad habits. But they did not speak ill of Kusumpur Pahari, nor of its residents and their qualities. As members of the historically discriminated Dalit caste, they expressed no rancour with the settlement or with India at large, choosing instead to speak of themselves as one of many poor families in Delhi and beyond challenged to secure a living. Satish talked about the unrelenting pressure of making ends meet and negotiating uncertainty, and when asked about what this required, he firmly planted his herding stick in the ground, shook it vigorously and uttered the Hindi word '*majbuti*', to mean inner strength and resolve. It was a word that other men of the settlement's more established families with relatively stable jobs could have used, and like Satish, without acknowledging properties of place, for example, the slum's vastly improved services and infrastructures in recent years and its proximity to opportunities and transport connections in prosperous South Delhi. Whatever its sources, the *majbuti* is fragile: in Satish's case put to the test when he badly hurt his leg and risked losing his job, but resolved by a R135000 (£1,500) loan he managed to obtain from his extended family to cover the medical costs and an employer's rare willingness to keep him on the books. With the couple's combined income just about covering monthly costs – kept down by negligible housing expenses due to illegal ownership and the availability of free water and electricity – the injury could have thrown the family into abject poverty, destroying Satish's *majbuti*.

On another outskirt of the settlement, we encountered a different kind of *majbuti* with its own fragilities. One morning, a tall man in his late sixties with a handlebar moustache, alerted by his barking dog tethered to a neem tree, approached us outside his two-storey house fronted by an ample compound and upstairs balcony. With a booming voice liberally peppered with colourful swear words, the man we called Prithviraj after the famous Indian film star he resembled, told us of arriving from Sindh forty years ago to a then tiny rural hamlet without services and occupying enough land to build a sizeable property. He spoke of bringing up two sons with his wife, developing a successful truck and construction business and becoming a respected and well-known local figure. Here was an early settler who had seen the settlement grow and become serviced, doing well for himself in the process. The conversation turned to *majbuti* when Prithviraj talked about the stress caused by his son's kidney failure, which led to the sale of the business to fund the treatment and kidney donation. While he acknowledged his financial losses and stresses, he said he drew strength from believing that *na jaan he na jahan he* ('where there is faith there is life'). If faith, drive and determination explained Prithviraj's positive outlook from his point of view, viewed from the outside, it was also clear that so did his standing in a community he had seen grow around him and which he described as cohesive and convivial. As we talked, a neighbour came by to ask for some leaves from his neem tree for an auspicious occasion, to which he consented with evident pride and satisfaction, his *majbuti* reinforced by his social status and positive sense of place. His was a life and outlook shielded from the poverty, overcrowding, domestic violence, petty crime and alcohol or drug abuse seen by others in the settlement as more typical of it.

This view of Kusumpur Pahari as anything but a cohesive community was expressed by three civically-minded friends who took us under their wing as we waited expectantly one morning for interlocutors in the large *maidan* (open space) on the settlement's outer perimeter, where young men gather to play games or smoke and drink, others cross to go into the woods or the city and women wait for the weekly water tankers to arrive. All three had intimate knowledge of the colony, having built their adult lives in it and taken an interest in local affairs. 'Aman' was a viewing agent for a local estate agent, 'Bimal' chauffeured for a middle-class South Delhi family and 'Rajiv' was a medical practitioner, having trained as a pharmacist and then under a qualified physician. The friends described families in Kusumpur Pahari as hard-working and lucky to enjoy free or low-rent accommodation and services in a location close to South Delhi, but they also spoke of a general lack of education, aspiration and skill in the settlement. A constant refrain from Aman was the problem of widespread alcohol and drug dependency among boys from an early age, exacerbated by truancy, peer pressure and the absence of working parents during the day. He cited substance dependency as a primary cause of youth underachievement and mental illness. Rajiv told us that only 2 per cent of addicts managed to go clean, even after attending clinics. Bimal suggested the authorities did not clamp down on the sale of drugs and alcohol in Delhi's slums because they took a cut from the trade.

All three men expressed an unparaded *majbuti* based on their effort to acquire skills, work hard and stay on the right side of the tracks in a challenging existential environment. They drew strength also from their interest in the wellbeing of the settlement. The medical practitioner, one among many local healers of varying qualifications and quality, shows this by charging the poorest residents less and by offering informed consultations and proven medicines, instead of ineffective placebos or cheap drugs dumped by pharmaceutical reps. Aman, possibly because of his involvement in the housing sector, warns his neighbours of the dangers of overcrowding and hazardous waste in the slum, and tries to organize them to build channels to get rid of stagnant grey water, without much success in sustaining effort because of the demands of other priorities or due to a loss of interest. Bimal's *majbuti* seemed to stem from a desire to mend bridges, as we saw from his patience with an angry addict who insisted on breaking into our conversation on the *maidan*, and from wanting to take us to a Sufi *dargah* (shrine) to show how in a moment of communalist violence in India a sanctuary in a slum opens its door to both Hindus and Muslims with mental and physical ailments. All three men expressed hope in the settlement as a space of convivial coexistence and reciprocal relations, premised on improved social aspiration and collaboration, but also the kind of civic interest they possessed.

Kusumpur Pahari has its share of strongarm *majbuti* tapping into India's communalist politics of resentment to restore Hindu piety, tradition and family respect as the ground of advancement in the settlement. It is typified by a young resident studying for an open degree we met who unhesitatingly identified 'culture' as the impediment, rather than provisions and opportunities that he saw as slowly improving through infrastructural and service investments in the slum by the municipal and national authorities. A member of Bajrang Dal, the youth wing of the militant Hindutva organization RSS where Modi started out, he quickly assembled other members of the Dal to meet us at a temple, forcing open gates that the Brahmin priest had shut for lunch. During an instructive hour of animated discussion within the group, peppered with respectful disagreement, laughter and hugs, and deference to the group leader, a consensus emerged accepting that while some social groups such as Dalits faced the disadvantages of discrimination, other Hindus left behind in India's slums suffered from the 'wrong' cultural values. The group had no doubt that afflictions such as unemployment, drug dependency and mental illness arose from the loss of traditional Hindu values of abstinence, respect for elders, family loyalty and religiousness, keeping young people from wrong kinds of friendship, deviancy and inactivity. Here was a martial *majbuti* typical of Hindutva nationalism, intolerant of the open and inclusive society, as we saw in the group's casual mockery of nearby JNU students, Muslims, liberals and opposers of India's new discriminatory citizenship laws. A club masculinity carried the young men's moral and political indignation towards modern Indian 'decay', poised for violence beyond the settlement, but held back by familiarities of place within it while othering the settlement's Muslim corner.

'*Shakti*'

The language of endurance in Kusumpur Pahari is gendered, as are responses to adversity. Once Aman asked us to note how everywhere men would idly play cards or get drunk, adding that for any change in the settlement you had to 'talk to the mothers'. The significance of women as carers, workers, providers and planners was amply evident. We saw how things cohered around them, despite the many harms they faced, including abuse from husbands and in-laws, money squandered by intoxicated husbands and sons, the restrictions of patriarchy and religion, the fatigue of duties from early morning to late night and the burden of seeing the family through difficulties. Under such pressure, we saw some women falling through the net as discussed below, but many more – supported by other women – endeavouring to provide, encourage and hope. The forbearance of women did not match the language of *majbuti*, but of *shakti*, a quiet strength of managing hardship and responsibility without animosity at the edge of deprivation and desperation. In their private lives of care, provision and persistence – always marred by uncertainty and injury – forms a worldliness set apart from nativist or liberal distinctions of affiliation and identification. It is a *shakti* that leans towards bridging divides through its practices of expansive connection even while serving in-group public and political attachments, its disposition of pragmatic relatedness ready to cross boundaries.

One example is provided by 'Gita', a woman in her late forties we met on the *maidan* carrying a new tyre for an autorickshaw. A long-term resident of Kusumpur Pahari, Gita lost her husband in 2016. Since his death, she had struggled to provide for her three children, saddled by a R1 lakh (£1,000) loan taken out by her husband to buy his autorickshaw, struggling to pay her daughter's school fees, unable to find sustained work as a maid in nearby gated communities and spurned by her husband's family. Yet *shakti* was scripted in her poise and voice, her plans to work with a driver to get the rickshaw back into service and her confidence in surviving her current difficulties. Hers had been a life of continual hardship faced with determination and optimism, reflected in her courage to overcome the fear of going to the woods before public toilet blocks arrived, parry her husband's drunken violence, bounce back from being laid off despite her good record and maintain her equanimity after finding drugs in her son's pockets. She had every reason to succumb if her circumstances got worse, yet it seemed as though her honed skills of survival would carry her through, she too helped by familiarities of place, including the possibility of sharing concerns and occasional favours with women in her part of the settlement, all from Bihar. Invited to meet some of the women near her home, we heard of their worries about crime, drugs, alcohol and boredom not that far away from their own lives, but also of their appreciation of infrastructural improvements and living next to familiar others in a space made more intimate by the interactions.

Walking away from a sobering encounter one day with two men who showed us a video clip in which a politician listed Kusumpur Pahari among planned slum clearances in Delhi, we were stopped by two mothers standing outside their homes near a *charpoy* (bed frame strung with tape) on which some young women played cards. With fluency, these inquisitive neighbours spoke of slum improvements, the educational and class discriminations facing the poor and the rights and wrongs of using (secular) 'India' or (religious) 'Hindustan' as the correct name of the nation, one playing up her Delhi background and the other her roots in rural Punjab. They readily agreed that 'despite our woes, laughter keeps us going and is good for stress', which to us seemed helped by the possibility of free banter with familiar others in the open, and the setting itself of their busy narrow street punctuated by many distractions (e.g. the arrival of a man selling winter quilts). The enrolment of space in forbearance leaning towards the convivial is most evident in the rituals of collecting drinking water. Once a week, but less frequently during warmer months of water shortage, groups of about twenty-five households collect water from a tanker crawling up narrow streets and causing traffic mayhem at stops where women wait with large blue containers. This waiting is largely silent, interrupted by occasional conversation, but it gives way to a frantic positioning, filling and removal of containers to instructions from one or two younger women wielding the tubes gushing with water, trying to minimize spillage while they fill the containers. The activity is focused, with each household anxious to receive its share and struggling to get its two heavy containers home along narrow alleys, but there is also an atmosphere of joint endeavour and humour (which can turn to frustration and anger when water is in short supply). The choreography of the roadside turned into shared public space is striking, offering the women small mercies to bear the stress of not having piped drinking water at home.

Shakti is a frustrating necessity for women from patriarchal families preventing them from seeking education and work beyond the settlement. We met a group of young women at a local sewing class which opened for two hours a day. They spoke with gratitude about its existence, despite the restricted hours and its location in a dark basement with old sewing machines at one end and weightlifting equipment at the other, doubling up as a gym. The group of two sisters and three friends from traditional Bihari families were just out of their teens, but already young wives and mothers who started the day at 5.00am with domestic and family chores and ended it late at night after seeing to the needs of the extended family for the following day. They kept home with the elder women of the family, required to ensure the wellbeing of its demanding – and often troubled – children and men. With surprising frankness, the women spoke of their hopes beyond domestic life – the pleasure after leaving school at an early age of learning sewing skills, meeting with other young women for an hour or two, hoping to find paid work locally as seamstresses, beauticians or shop assistants, dreaming of sleeping longer at the rare visits to their village and visiting places beyond the settlement. Theirs is a stifled life, yet we sensed little rancour, only a certain steeliness glimpsed when the two sisters spoke of not fearing local drunks and layabouts, and fighting off youths who once attacked their brother. Outside the home, the women shirked ascribed roles, their relation with 'tradition' quite different from that of the Bajrang Dal men engaged in a war of resentment and blame.

Someone who has long worked with women in Kusumpur Pahari is Sonia Verma, an educator who has lived in Kusumpur Pahari since 1974 and seen a collection of flimsy shelters turn into a settlement of solid houses, commercial activity and public services and spaces. Chair of the Delhi branch of the All-India Democratic Women's Association, Sonia has since 1990 run a Rotary Club creche caring for the children of working mothers and teaching them basic language and counting skills. Having got to know many women, she has extensive knowledge of their lives and trials, confirming to us the daily reality of long and arduous hours punctuated by abuse from husbands demanding money to feed a habit, often causing bouts of depression, listlessness and distraction that the women themselves diagnose as passing physical ailments rather than mental disorders requiring medical attention. With some hope Sonia also spoke of an emerging *shakti* among the settlement's younger women to test domestic boundaries, ensure their children's education, connect through the social media and explore their rights as women. Common to the variegations of *shakti*, however, seemed the practised art of enduring a tested life on which so much depends, one leaning towards convivial relations with others and the world at large rather than animosity, helped by familiarities of place and neighbourly affinities.

Forbearance Forestalled

Forbearance hovers on a knife's edge, never far from descending into desperation and resentment. In Kusumpur Pahari's vacant lots and open spaces such as the *maidan* and its adjacent woods, it is easy to find idle men, and occasionally women, whose life courses have been altered by the smallest or spiralling mishaps. The men wander alone, stand quietly in groups, huddle around fires, or play cards on the ground, often surrounded by the smell of alcohol or weed. The younger men seem idle because of lost chances of education, work and ambition due to drug or drink dependency from an early age, while the older men appear to have additional reasons including troubled behavioural histories and family circumstances, or bouts of misfortune. In the field it was hard to know how badly these individuals (and others shut indoors) suffered from severe disorders such as psychosis and schizophrenia. This seemed likely from the men's visual appearances and our informants talking about the combined effects of severe hardship, psychological damage and substance abuse. We often heard about widespread alcohol and drug dependency in the settlement and its manifestation in depression, aggression and paranoia, all left untreated due to lack of awareness, resources or inclination. It seemed common to simply live with the symptoms, persevere somehow, cleave to a life however stripped down, hoping for better days with the help of mothers, sisters and wives.

Yet in Kusumpur Pahari (and most other informal settlements), these men are not avoided or stigmatized, as they might be in more prosperous or anonymous neighbourhoods. They are accepted, perhaps with some caution and disapproval, but with no hint of rejection from the community. Their right to belong, perhaps because they are familiar to so many in a place in which it is known how easy it is to fall or fail, seems taken as given, even if there is little sympathy for the idleness, misbehaviour and damage linked to addiction. As we listened to Aman and Rajiv speak about how rarely the mentally ill consulted clinics or nearby hospitals such as Safdarjung, a man with fiery eyes and arms covered in tattoos approached our group. After demurring for a moment, the man interrupted to ask why we did not want to hear from someone like him, and as we took in his question, he shouted out that life would improve if the settlement had drinking water, employment, a hospital and a crematorium. He said that although Safdarjung hospital was nearby, the poor kept away knowing that many people did not come out alive, including surgery patients and new born babies. He told us how, instead of going to hospital when his father broke his hands and legs for his substance addiction, he turned to Shiva, the Hindu god also worshipped by bacchanalians. We listened warily and when Bimal dared to blame the easy availability of alcohol in the settlement, the man told him to shut up, declaring that people from all over India and the state benefitted from this. He shouted to Bimal to go home, while Amal quietly reminded him of the value of listening to different points of view. Clearly disturbed, he stood his ground, while Bimal, Aman and the doctor looked on, more embarrassed by his outburst than fearful of him. There was no hint of aversion or stigmatization in their response, and as the man angrily walked off, the three friends offered no apology or comment to us, accustomed to living with all manner of familiar others in a small settlement.

The postures of fallen women are different. One bitterly cold morning, one of three women huddled in blankets around a fire in an opening between an elementary school and public toilet block called out to ask who we were and what we wanted. Explaining that we were looking into wellbeing and belonging in poor settlements, she immediately let us know that women like her had nothing – no work, no husbands, no income, not enough food despite government rations, no help from their children who just roamed out of school or work, no support from anyone in the colony or beyond. Rhetorically, she said that death was the way out of her predicament. In that moment, the three women had little more than each other's company, the meagre warmth of the fire and a place in the busy opening where they could watch the world go by. They were angry and desperate, scornful of politicians who simply showed up for their votes at election time, of women who priced them out of the labour market by accepting low wages, of a schooling system requiring children to have private tuition to succeed and of husbands and sons who simply added to their burden. One of them looked on with indifference bordering on contempt when we apologized for not being able to help them, while a third women muttered, as she walked away from the conversation, 'what remains when a man runs off into the woods with someone else and never comes back? My life is destroyed'. She was referring to being abandoned by her husband.

There could be no doubt about the plight of these materially and mentally exhausted women living on the edge of survival. Yet behind the words of desperation lay an obligation to provide. The vocal woman spoke of her desire to prevent her two orphaned nephews from being taken into care, and she asked Gunjesh to help with an application to access disability funds to help educate one of the nephews with a mental handicap. We sensed a similar tenacity in the other two women having to provide for their own dependents from nothing, but especially in a fourth woman standing beside a stool on which were laid out few small bags of sweets, biscuits and savouries. She could not have earned much from selling the items to primary children with only a few spare rupees, but in her dignified appearance and initiative lay signs of not giving up. Quietly she explained how she lost her job as a maid after visiting her village, yet still having to provide for four children. One of them, a girl no older than 16, stood nearby cradling her baby and behaved in ways that indicated a mental illness, while another daughter, we were told, needed her marriage to be funded, while a son sporadically brought in money as a day labourer. We were baffled by the family's ability to survive, but not by the woman's quiet tenacity. Hesitantly we asked how she managed to cope, and pointing to her stool of threadbare goods, she said 'this is all I can do'. Unlike the fallen men of the settlement, the fallen women cannot escape obligations that keep them both sane and desperate.

The significance of this responsibility struck home one day when we stood with patients and carers in long queues at the Institute of Human Behaviour and Allied Sciences (IHBAS),

Delhi's renowned mental health hospital. It was clear that without the relatives who live with the ill, nurture and cajole them, keep them and others safe and seek out remedies, the patients would succumb. Mothers and wives in Kusumpur Pahari usually fail to get a troubled son or husband into a medical clinic, making their role in keeping them afloat even more pivotal, along with whatever local affordances were available. During our days there we only glimpsed the lives of people on the edge of desperation, but it seemed that living in a community of known others and shared spaces helped to prevent their wholesale decline and alienation. The idle youths, abandoned women, mentally ill and intoxicated men are part of the collective life of the settlement. They are not ostracized or condemned, and there are many open spaces for them to gather, socialize and mingle with other residents. In such spaces, they pass the time of day, find company, look out for useful information and opportunity, claim their membership of a wider community. The ecology of the settlement, with its variegated economic and social structure, dense cohabitation, free services, bustling commerce, extended families, porosities of private and public life and spaces of comingling, keeps the most vulnerable from the extremes of abjection in places like Yamuna Pushta, where the habitat conspires against wellbeing.

Abjection, Flight, Organized Care

One place where the homeless gather is along the banks of the river Yamuna in Old Delhi cleared of slums in 2004 by the Municipal Corporation in preparation for the 2010 Commonwealth Games. In this space, the bare habitat, similar biographies and life conditions, and multiple deprivations reinforce the mental and physical fragility of the homeless as well as their sense of unbelonging. Typically, the men of various ages sheltering under flimsy bamboo structures covered in cloth and plastic have become homeless after a family feud, accident or illness, or after years of poverty or migration from city to city and job to job. Often, they do not possess the identity documents needed to access state rations and income or welfare support, under the shadow of tightening discriminations of citizenship by the BJP government. Camped out amid sparse trees and bare ground, the men are either too incapacitated to work or they manage to find work as day labourers for 3–4 days a month, pushing carts, pulling hand rickshaws, sorting rubbish, working at construction sites, filling in at festivals and weddings. Their earnings are meagre and sporadic, confirmed by the men we met walking about to keep warm or huddled around acrid fires burning plastic waste. They spoke of 'getting by', waiting for 'a turn in fortune', 'not having the option to kill myself', expectant of drink or drugs and a meagre meal at lunchtime from charitable organizations. They have access to water taps, toilets and occasional medical help provided by NGOs, alone in each other's company and distractions such as games and inexpensive films shown in two tent cinemas laid out with mattresses, and trying to avoid the petty crime and violence bred by addiction in the camp.

The homeless find themselves isolated, stigmatized and stripped bare, unaided by the habitat of makeshift and rugged shelters, litter and smoke from burning plastic, barren landscape dissected by a large overground water pipe, wandering dogs, abject mornings changing into loud drunken evenings. The habitat, apart from its rudimentary services, two cinemas, few trees and river bank, and one or two food *dhabas* and tea stalls, is a temporary camp and not a settlement with spatial affordances. It does not help in the fine balance between finding the presence of body and mind to stay secure and resorting to distractions that provide relief from the stresses of bare life, including the loss of self-worth after rejection by kith and kin and abuse from the authorities and public at large. The days mix alertness and numbness after years of street life, deprivation, loneliness, maltreatment and addiction, and of living with undiagnosed mental disorders such as anxiety, depression and paranoia. Our mentor Gufran was in no doubt from his involvement with the homeless about their scandalously underreported high rates of mortality and severe mental illness, occasionally rectified by NGOs in the field reporting a death or taking a very ill person to a clinic. He was clear that Delhi's many homeless people misdiagnose their ailments, lack family and peer care and are reluctant to seek help, afraid of being abused on public transport and by hospital sentries and medical staff. For Gufran the public authorities show no interest in their mental and physical health except during a public incidence, when they are rounded up or punished.

The homeless in Yamuna Pushta and countless other spaces in Delhi where they can shelter are stretched to breaking point, surviving through exceptional resolve or the meagre provisions and care of overstretched NGOs. One lunchtime, beside a queue for free food from a Gurdwara van, we spoke to a tall middle-aged man standing apart. In perfect English, he told us about how he left school in Calcutta to work because of his father's gambling habit, eventually managing a food store in Lucknow and then moving to Delhi in 1997, where after a 'mishap' and 'fragility' he ended up in Yamuna Pushta ten years ago. 'Kapil' did not explain these causes, but admitted to feeling alone and lonely, though also lucky to be housed in one of the very few permanent shelters in Yamuna Pushta and to have access to free food, basic services and medicine for his asthma. Helped, he spoke well of his cohabitants at Yamuna Pushta despite his class and caste difference, mentioning the meagre but meaningful ways of supporting each other. He offered firm ideas about how things could be improved for the homeless, suggesting that the offer of in-situ medical care for the mentally ill, and learning opportunities to help steer the homeless away from drink and apathy, would make a difference. Kapil affirmed that he would never lose hope, confident that the medicine and identity documents Gufran was obtaining for him would allow him to return to work after 18 months of absence because of his asthma. We were unsure of this, yet remained struck by his stoicism and optimism, undoubtedly explained by his own biography, but also by his unusual access to free shelter, food, services and medical care. Personhood and care wove into his self-poise and sensitivity towards his cohabitants in this unforgiving environment.

Yamuna Pushta is a place for single men. One exception is 'Devi', a woman living in a makeshift tent set apart from other shelters. She showed the same tenacity and generosity as Kapil, despite having to survive without access to sheltered housing and care. Devi called out to us as we walked down a grassy bank to the river, warning us that we were on ground where people defecated. We turned back to talk to her outside a tent with a small enclosed area at the front, where a woman cooked on an open fire and an unwell boy played. Devi offered us tea and apologized for not being able to offer us chairs to sit on. With a kind of survivor calm she told us about her tragic story of having to sell her home a decade before to fund treatment for her cancer (initially in Bangalore and latterly at All India Institute of Medical Sciences (AIIMS) in South Delhi), seeing her husband dying from an accident around the same time, looking after her nephew we saw playing when her sister and her husband died crossing a busy road, and regularly missing her cancer appointments at AIIMS, unable to afford the bus fare and daunted by the 28 km walk to and from the hospital. Devi had sold her kidney to make ends meet and to ensure that her nephew was not taken into care. After a long period of wandering from place to place, she found Yamuna Pushta where she could get free food and basic services and hope for some income from her teenage son working as a day labourer in Old Delhi. Devi's *shakti* was like Gita's in Kusumpur Pahari, manifest in the narration of her life in the active voice as a series of steps taken without rancour and self-regard to face one tragedy after another, yet without the surroundings that Gita can draw something from.

Flight/Faith

The field observations of the left-behind in Delhi show how relations of wellbeing and belonging are embedded in the grammar of enduring hardship, contiguous others and the lived habitat. Woven into this grammar are fantasies of flight and faith that project a redemptive future from the arduous present as a way of bearing the load and imagining another community. These redemptive fantasies are personal and private, distant from the political mobilizations of nation, though temperamentally closer to those not interested in fellowship on the back of others. Most of the homeless men in Yamuna Pushta look for temporary relief in drink or drugs to escape their dire conditions. They are carried away yet damaged by the respite from the tortures of daily life and mind, as vividly encapsulated in Aman Sethi's (2012) journal of a rough-sleeping construction worker in Delhi, Michele Lancione's (2019) intimate portraits of drug addicts in Bucharest, and Fast and Moyer's (2018) ethnography of the flight-worlds of homeless youths in Dar es Salaam. They drift into forgetting and fantasizing, the substances providing a way of putting up with extreme and unrelenting misery in the dangerous and unforgiving camp. There are few men like Kapil who can hope without intoxication, or those with good health setting out early in clothes washed in drains emptying into the river to look for work across Old Delhi. In the bare landscape of idleness, the two cinemas play their part, showing popular films that distract the viewers keeping warm under blankets on threadbare mattresses as they drift in and out of sleep and the dramas unfolding on screen. Aided or not, fantasy is central to the psychology of endurance in Yamuna Pushta, giving small glimpses of another place for men whose energies are consumed by finding a way to simply survive the day. They have no interest in fantasies of the pure nation and its authentic subjects, only in flightpaths that can alleviate their suffering and affirm their right to exist.

Fantasies are no less important for the well-off residents of Delhi's slums, though not to escape poverty. The fantasy could be for somewhere offering a more exciting life. In a slum at the edge of an authorized resettlement colony in West Delhi, we spent some time with a family of cowherds known to Gunjesh. After living there for 30 years, the family has become prosperous and runs a dairy, owning a herd of 100 cows, four commercial trucks and shacks along a canal skirting the slum rented out to the very poor. The extended family lives modestly in a brick dwelling to which more storeys have been pieced together over the years, facing a yard with two small goat sheds that narrows into a lane leading out of the slum, where their cows roam freely on the main road to Wazirpur metro station. The family has accumulated considerable assets and runs a thriving business, yet its members do not see themselves as rich or any different from the other residents of the slum. They worry about interference from the authorities and about the welfare of their cows, and they work hard, starting the day well before dawn and ending it late after milking the cows, cleaning and delivering the churns, driving the feed trucks and seeing to family matters. But while the head of family quietly counts his blessings, his eldest son 'Rohit', in his late twenties who runs the business, dreams of a different and less taxing life. At our meetings, Rohit would quickly tire with our questions about the family's history and sense of place and about the ways of the slum and its residents, wanting only to talk about visiting London. He would ask how much a holiday would cost, where he could stay, how he could obtain a visa, what he would eat, what there was to see, whether he would be allowed to stay to work – all questions easily answered by browsing the web or asking a close friend of his who lives in London. Perhaps this was his way of finding common ground with a Briton or evading 'dull' conversation about wellbeing and belonging in the slum, but the sparkle in his eyes in dreaming of London and his declarations of 'being bored as a doctor of cows' betrayed something else. For Rohit, 'stuck' with a young wife and two small children and a trade with no let up, London had become a fantasy object, a place to fulfil his desire for a carefree and adventurous life. Wazirpur offered no flight, other than in the literal sense of Rohit and his friends flying pigeons from the rooftop and seeing them capture rival pigeons with the help of calls, claps and whistles. In much the same way, a bright and vocal cousin of his completing high school dodged our questions about slum life by enthusing about on-line courses and motivational gurus that would help him fulfil his quest to become a successful 'network' entrepreneur. For him, too, the dream of a life away from the traditional work of tending cows in the city seemed essential, even if it made a prosperous present feel unbearable.

Most slum dreams, however, are less fanciful and more grounded. In Kusumpur Pahari, residents spoke of their desire for piped drinking water, stable work, better education and welfare, a future free from the threat of eviction, and escape from domestic and patriarchal restrictions. These were not flights of fantasy but quests for the means to a more secure life, yet surrounded by temples, mosques, shrines and religious decorations everywhere we walked, we wondered if faith and prayer provided some escape from the trials of everyday hardship. It seemed not. Rarely did we see people praying or stopping at roadside shrines, and at the Hindu temple we visited to talk to the Brahmin *pandit* (priest), meet with the Bajrang Dal group, or write field notes, we occasionally saw people coming to make an offering and be on their way again. It was the temple's courtyard that was more visited as a space of doing and gathering, occupied by the *pandit* cooking his lunch, people preparing for a wedding, other Hindu organizations displaying their teachings and groups meeting under its large shady tree. The *pandit* described half the settlement's residents as believers – by rote rather than conviction – and the remaining half as 'ungodly and uncouth', interested only in 'chasing drink', 'killing and eating animals' and 'working, eating and quarrelling'. He was quick to tell us that he kept to himself, did not eat with locals, lived elsewhere and looked forward to being moved on to a different temple. Detached, he probably had little idea of what religion meant for his parishioners, but in all our conversations with residents about their wellbeing and sense of place, we rarely sensed that in faith was sought flight or cure.

There was one notable exception. This was the Sufi shrine where Bimal took us, in the courtyard of his neighbour's house. It was a clean and tranquil tiled space, in which devotional music was playing and sayings were displayed of a Sufi mystic whose effigy lies in an inner room covered in flowers and photos. On Sunday evenings the shrine, which has existed for over 20 years, opens its doors to people suffering from various physical and mental illnesses, frequently individuals for whom medical treatments have not worked. The shrine's medium, a man with bright and smiling eyes following in the footsteps of his father who created the space, spoke of visitors being cured of renal problems, extreme anger, manic depression and infertility after visiting the *dargah*. When we asked about what treatment he offered, he replied that after briefly answering a pre-submitted written question, he would leave the troubled individuals and their families to pray, chant and 'receive the spiritual force'. We had no way of verifying his claims, but left persuaded by the special atmosphere of the shrine, the medium's healing touch and the trust of the afflicted and their families in the power of mystical experience. We discovered that the *dargah* was known across Delhi, attracted people from all faiths and did not charge a penny, its reputation resting on the stories told about the special powers of the medium. It is one of many Sufi shrines in India sought out in large numbers for spiritual healing, but unexceptional: very much part of the slum, opening only for a few hours every week because the family is poor and must earn a living (the medium drives for a family in South Delhi), and integrated into a neighbourhood of shared existential challenges and experiences. Bimal wanted us to know that the *dargah*, visited by Hindus and Muslims, epitomized a culture of rubbing along in the settlement.

Pratap Sharan is a senior clinical psychiatrist at AIIMS Delhi, in charge of the Institute's public health and community psychiatry services. When we met, he admitted that slum residents rarely came to AIIMS for treatment because they lacked time and resources, mis-recognized or ignored mental symptoms and feared hospitals. We expected him to suggest ways of getting the poor to specialist clinics and hospitals through better awareness campaigns and by making visits more conducive, but surprisingly he suggested another course. Accepting that Indians from all castes and religions regularly visit Sufi shrines to cure mental illness through prayer, song and religious consultation, Professor Sharan suggested that the medical profession should recognize faith-healing as 'a significant component of India's public mental health regime' and acknowledge shrines as centres of spiritual health and rehabilitation. Through his involvement in Brighupathi Singh's research on Sufi shrines, he had come to the conclusion that a therapeutic way forward, given the popularity of faith-healing and the reluctance of the poor to visit hospitals, would be for clinicians to go to slums, working as equals with faith-healers to holistically tackle the multiple dimensions of mental disorder. He thought local schools could double up as neighbourhood healing centres, accepted by all parties as neutral spaces. These were radical ideas, coming from a leading clinician steeped in the science of psychiatric care, but one alert to lived experiences of poverty and ground vernaculars of diagnosis. Here was a very different acknowledgement of faith and its therapeutic alliances from Hindutva political mobilizations of faith for discord.

Organized Care

The homeless endure physical and mental illnesses without the means to find remedies, facing inevitable deterioration save for the intervention of a stretched non-governmental infrastructure of care. This support is far from easy to obtain. According to Gufran, of the 200,000 homeless people in Delhi, only 5 per cent manage to find temporary or permanent accommodation in 285 shelters – largely in Old Delhi – authorized by the Delhi government and run by NGOs. Most of the shelters house single men or women and young families in separate dormitories, and a handful of recovery centres offer treatment for drug addiction or physical and mental illnesses. In addition to the night shelters in Yamuna Pushta, we looked at two housing compounds at Urdu Park and Meena Bazaar near Old Delhi's historic Jama Masjid, and two recovery centres, one for women in the slum of Kabir Basti, and the other for men at Yamuna Bank along the busy, multiple-lane, Monastery Ring Road. Though rudimentary, with the NGOs running them constrained by limited financial and human resources as well as bureaucratic impediments such as having to tender regularly for government concessions, the shelters and recovery centres offer a glimpse of the institutional structures of care that keep the homeless afloat.

The container-like shelters on the upper level of Yamuna Pushta are no more than dormitories that men queue outside every evening for a free bed on a first-come, first-served basis, one of them permanently housing a small number of elderly men like Kapil, left to wander during the day. They are night shelters filled with beds in serried rank, instructions pinned inside the entrance, and not a lot more else. By contrast, the very best housing shelters, such as those at Jama Masjid, are located in enclosed compounds that feel like small settlements. In these shelters run by SPYM, an NGO that started out working with drug addicts, the fortunate few with acute circumstances, who are allowed to stay for a fixed period, live in single-sex or family dormitories kitted out with electricity, television, decorations and spaces for socializing, and have access to toilets, washing facilities, a kitchen, play areas and the shelter of greenery in the secure compound. The residents are provided with bedding, clothing and some medical care but not food, which they are expected to buy and cook for themselves. Drugs and alcohol are forbidden and during the day children are expected to attend school while their parents are helped to find work in the bustling economy around Jama Masjid. The compounds are clean and pleasant, in the mornings offering classes and lunch to the youngest children. The shelters have the feel of a safe and homely environment, run by staff who treat the homeless with respect, counselling them in various ways, informing them of their rights, helping them to build their self-respect and confidence, making them feel protected, and enabling them to support each other. The contrast with the homeless people squatting outside the compounds could not be starker. The SPYM staff we spoke to accepted that residents find it hard to find and maintain jobs, change their ways and acquire the confidence and means to leave the dormitories. They were realistic about what a short period of safe shelter can achieve, but sure that providing longer-term housing and care to the homeless would tangibly improve their wellbeing, capabilities and survival without stigmatization and abandonment.

We caught a glimpse of what they meant. At a shelter in Urdu Park, Gufran introduced us to 'Zeinab', a homeless young mother who has become a paid volunteer and drug counsellor at the shelter. With uncanny economy and dignity, Zeinab recounted her story. She started out as a child beggar at Jama Masjid because her father, a rickshaw puller, could not earn enough money. She fell into drug and alcohol addiction, coming close to becoming a sex-worker, when she met a Hindu who she married and had three children with. In 2013 their home in the faraway resettlement slum of Bawana was destroyed in a fire that also killed her infant son. Not long after, her one-year-old daughter was raped by someone who her husband chased down and punished. Advised by the police that an internal medical inspection might kill her daughter, Zeinab decided against one, which meant that a rape case could not be pursued. Let off, the rapist filed a case against her husband for the beating, which left Zeinab having to find R20,000 (£200) to free her husband from prison. In turn, the paltry R100,000 (£1000) promised for the loss of her home and her son was only paid after she petitioned Delhi's Chief Minister in person. The upheavals led to the break-up of her marriage. Zeinab had survived because a unique combination of *shakti* and *majbuti* had carried her through her litany of misfortune and her efforts to overcome addiction to provide for her children. Nothing can diminish the strength of her determination, but it is Urdu Park and NGO care that have made for a new and more secure life. The shelter has provided Zeinab with the earnings to bring up her children and support the rest of her family, the lifestyle, friendships and community to move past painful chapters of the past, and professional help to prepare for the future (lately as a Muslim without a birth certificate having to prove her Indian origins as required by the Modi government's discriminatory National Register of Citizens). The significance of her changed circumstances enabling rehabilitation struck home as we stood in the fading evening light watching Zeinab gently attend to her baby boy and daughter under the shade of a tree as the call to prayers rang out from Jama Masjid.

Recovery shelters provide another lifeline to the homeless, again all too meagrely but through no fault of the NGOs running them. The shelter beside the busy highway at Yamuna Bank, run by Gufran's organization CES, is a fenced compound with grassed areas and a volleyball pitch in front of two long metal dormitories. One dormitory is a night shelter for a hundred homeless men, like the ones at Yamuna Pushta, and the other one houses fifty homeless patients with physical or mental ailments, with areas sectioned off for patients with HIV and infectious TB. Little in the arrangements of the latter dormitory gave away its function other than the sight of unwell individuals lying down. It did not look like a medical ward, only a collection of beds in an undisinfected space with minimal comforts and provisions. The patients, typically suffering from accidents, breathing difficulties and kidney or liver problems, waited for the attention of a peripatetic nurse or doctor. Mixed in were a handful of patients with mental illnesses offered respite and medicines prescribed by hospitals that have seen them. We found more mental health patients at the homeless women's recovery shelter in Kabir Basti, here too, mixed in with general patients in an equally crowded and basic dormitory. Located in a leafy compound with a large amphitheatre at the back, this shelter is run by an NGO called DUSIB, staffed by a manager with qualifications in pharmacy and counselling, a nurse and some social and general workers. The recovery shelter receives mentally ill homeless women sent by medical centres such as IHBAS or picked up by the police, and offers them prescribed medication, occasional psychiatric support, and a daily schedule of food and hygiene, exercise and rehabilitation, and basic skills training. The women tend to suffer from psychosis, schizophrenia and the anxieties and traumas of deprivation and abuse on the streets, bewildered, alone and undervalued when they come to the shelter. They need sustained counselling and care that the shelter is unable to provide, but the care and medicine on offer provides a glimpse of possibility and worth destroyed on the streets. The women are allowed to stay until deemed fit to leave, supported by work placements in local enterprises and advice on where they can stay once released.

The manager was candid about the success of the DUSIB recovery shelter, sure that its holistic approach had helped half the patients to get better, but also aware of the impediments to rehabilitation, from rudimentary conditions in the shelter and gaps in its medical and psychiatric care, to the all too easy return to decline and desperation once women leave the shelter. She considered the support available in Delhi for widespread mental illness among the homeless as a drop in the ocean, compounded by laws that prevent recovery centres from providing treatment if the homeless cannot supply documents to prove their identity and homelessness, which is almost always the case. Like Gufran and others with direct experience, she knew what needs to change, including the provision of many more and better resourced treatment centres, longer and more holistic periods of care, a post-recovery infrastructure of reintegration into work and housing, initiatives to restore the capabilities and self-worth of the homeless, and permission to treat illnesses without crippling layers of bureaucracy. In the absence of such a network, under-resourced NGOs in the field remain the sole, all too stretched, source of medical treatment, legal support and basic necessities. As we ended our days with Gufran in the cold night air of Meena Bazaar, he asked with frustration why public institutions insisted on seeing documentary evidence that the vast majority of the homeless did not possess, when it was clear that they lived on the street and were in need of medicine, rations, income and other state entitlements for the very poor. Standing next to a woman who had pressed him all evening for extra blankets, he called out to Gunjesh and me as we walked towards the metro station: 'they are already the children of India. Do children need to prove who they are when they return home?'. He could just as well have been talking about the millions in India caught out by the new National Register of Citizens that requires documents proving birth or residence in India prior to 2015, offering exceptions to all religious groups except Muslims unable to provide the evidence. Under pressure from a Hindu nationalist government seeing no wrong in ethnic, religious and cultural cleansing, the law has become a biopolitical weapon against those deemed unwanted in India.

On that last evening, we had observed a mobile clinic for the homeless in one corner of the busy market in Meena Bazaar next to Jama Masjid. The clinic encapsulated the contradictions of care for the homeless. Run as a joint venture between IHBAS and the NGO Ashre Abhikar Abhyan, the clinic opened twice a week for four hours, attended by NGO social workers, a general practitioner and clinical psychiatrist, a magistrate and some police officers (even though the 2017 mental health act allows a nominated representative of a homeless person to be present instead of the police). That evening, under bright torches the officers verified the documents of the assembled patients already registered at IHBAS hospital or at recovery centres, constantly consulting with the social workers. In the meantime, the doctors saw three categories of patient in succession: addicts, general health patients and the mentally ill. The process was swift, formal and medicalized. Seated under a makeshift canopy, the doctors rushed through two queues of addicts and general patients, checking their prescriptions and records, before letting them collect medicines from the back of the medical van. The mental health patients, brought from recovery shelters so as to avoid long waits at IHBAS, were the last to be seen, their two to three hours of waiting in the cold reduced to a few minutes with the psychiatrist, who after a few basic questions put to them or their social workers, scribbled copious notes in their files and talked at length with the magistrate about how much at risk they were. Perhaps the consultations were simply progress check-ups (in fact we saw no new prescriptions written) but we could not help thinking that in the rush of time and the demands of bureaucracy, the vital empathy that underpins psychiatric care was absent. The patients went away as silently and disoriented as they had arrived – gazed at, recorded and assessed, but not counselled with care and interest as individuals with complex and multiple afflictions. Yet, without the mobile clinic, the homeless would have no access to qualified psychiatrists prescribing free medication, and estranged from their families, they can count on the care of the NGO staff who know them and work collaboratively with the doctors and diverse officials, for once all in one place to speed up the process. The collaborations stripped of their biopolitical aims give a glimpse of the structures of care that could begin to treat the most vulnerable citizens of India in a meaningful way.

Situated Affordances

In all the states of subjectivity and belonging discussed so far, there are strong spatial mediations. The condition of the homeless in Yamuna Pushta is worse and more isolated than that of the people living in the shelters at Meena Bazaar and Urdu Park, which offer possibilities of respite and reconnection from care provided, the decent state of the compounds, services and dormitories, and opportunities for convivial cohabitation and learning. The densities of cohabitation may be similar, but the social outcomes are very different, because of the affordances of place. The habitat at Yamuna Pushta makes for a bare and isolated existence, its meagre *dhabas* and cinemas, acrid fires and stilted conversations providing fleeting relief. But for the rudimentary services located on its upper strip, Yamuna Pushta is a space of tents, trees, open fires, rubbish heaps and scavenging animals, and the homeless are reduced to relying on an inner reserve and supportive relations that are hard to find. Their prospects depend on the serendipities of securing temporary work, taking flight, helping each other and finding aid for their physical and mental afflictions. Place does not take up any of the slack and, if anything, adds to their difficulties through its bleak and monotonous landscape, rudimentary infrastructures and flimsy shacks, absent social and commercial life, and menacing and unpredictable atmosphere. The line in the habitat between descent and bare survival is drawn by the availability of running water and free toilets and NGO provisions of food, shelter, medical care and empathy.

This is not the case in Kusumpur Pahari, where the gradual evolution of a slum of impromptu tents into a poor neighbourhood of solid buildings, commercial life, social variegation and public services has lightened the load of its residents, though in the differentiated ways already discussed. Over the years, households have seen the arrival of piped water and metred electricity to their homes, tankers more regularly delivering drinking water and municipal initiatives to provide communal toilet blocks and taps, street lighting, rubbish collection, a clinic (*mohalla*) and security cameras. There remain problems of erratic water and electricity supply, poor sanitation and waste disposal, and inadequate health and welfare services, but the impediments of infrastructural and service lack are far fewer than in the past, when meeting basic needs absorbed vast amounts of time, energy and cost, at the expense of the well-being of residents and convivial social relations. The communal improvements have helped to alleviate the stresses of living in small and densely packed dwellings in an overcrowded settlement with many intrusions on privacy. Similarly, there have been marked improvements in the quality of public services, especially in the last few years under a pro-poor Delhi municipal government. The colony is a stone's throw away from the new Vasant Vihari metro station, which has considerably enlarged the radius of the labour and higher education market, while the nearby Sarvodaya Vidyalaya secondary school has implemented policy reforms designed to improve the curriculum and quality of teaching and care in state schools. The opportunity now exists for slum children to access decent secondary education locally, which might help to discourage boys from roaming the streets while their parents are out at work and attract girls from traditional families held back for domestic duties.

A general lack of elementary and primary education in the settlement is partially offset by NGO initiatives. One is the Rotary Club creche run by Sonia Verma, which strives to educate the children of working mothers. The creche offers classes in basic language and life skills, encouraging a taste for education, while enabling mothers to go out to work, reassured that their children are in the hands of a woman with extensive teaching experience, knowledge of the community and commitment to community empowerment. At the other end of the settlement is another NGO venture that teaches children aged three to eight basic Hindi and English, reading and writing, and maths in preparation for entry into state schools. The school's approach is to nest the formal classes in many activities of play and creativity such as drawing and storytelling, ending the morning with free lunch. The success of the school is reflected in the enthusiasm of the fifty-odd children, the balanced curriculum, the dedication of the principal who is from Kusumpur Pahari, the many posters on the walls and the cleanliness of the classroom space. Run by the Ritinjali NGO, the school was established in 2003 by the patron of an elite private school in nearby Vasant Kunj who heard from its gardeners that children at Kusumpur Pahari had little access to primary education. After an indifferent beginning, the school has become popular, and *in loco parentis* the teachers help the children to obtain official documents, encourage them to continue schooling, advise them against alcohol and drugs and protect them from violence at home.

Separated by a large and neglected muddy field from Sonia Verma's creche is a training venture also funded by Delhi's Rotarians, brightening a forlorn landscape with colourful murals of people in training by a Delhi street arts group. Established over 25 years ago, the centre offers young women free courses in basic Hindi and English, computing, sewing and beauty treatment, along with language and computing classes for children. It is run by a professional staff of seven people and managed by a retired Wing Commander. Demand for the courses is high and they help local women to acquire useful labour market skills and strengthen their voice in the family and community. The Wing Commander took no time to tell us that 'teaching a girl is teaching a family' and that women lay at the heart of communal life in poor settlements. He felt it important that organizations like the Rotary Club play their part in empowering women in this way and also by sponsoring savings groups to ensure that 'money squandered by husbands still leaves the women with something for the family'. The scale of NGO initiatives in Kusumpur Pahari for children and women is modest in relation to the need for basic education and training, but the centres are an important symbol of institutional provisions that far exceed their remit. They offer free professional services to help residents – often women and children unable to travel beyond the settlement – not only to develop valuable skills and capabilities, but also to play a part in raising aspirations and improving communal life.

There are also affordances of local social density. Consider alone those of public space, arising out of its coproduction, intense occupancy and informal relational interactions. In the settlement's many outside living rooms, the gathered intimacies thread into subjectivity through routines of visual recognition and familiarity, chats around fires, water tankers and street corners, walks to the *maidan* to loiter or play cards, cricket and hopscotch, time passed on charpoys, outside shops and in alleyways, calls to neighbours across roof terraces and common experience of the same thunder of landing planes, smells and visual landscape, and choreography of vehicles, animals and people in negotiation. States of mind, dispositions towards others and senses of belonging are shaped in a very public micro-geography in which the 'neighbours, the relatives, the people you live with ... share the same space, breathe the same air, live the same contradictions' (Rechtman, 2017: 134). This is not a micro-geography of sameness, but one of potentiality, weaving into subjectivity in different ways, depending on its balances of menace and assurance, and the biographies and states of wellbeing of individual residents. Similar lives led in the same open space in Yamuna Pushta find only threats and subtractions in its micro-geography, not enhancements. But in the dense heterogeneities of Kusumpur Pahari, the culture of public space helps to level difference, build a shared sense of place, manage anxiety and boredom, suspend private cares, share information and favours and facilitate sociability. To the monotony, uncertainty and stress of daily existence, an outdoors brimming with familiar markers of coexistence and private life 'spilling from the house into the street' (Das, 2017: 195) offers opportunities for comparison, reassurance and distractions (Simone, 2018). Over the days we would see the man who had warned us about the threat of slum eviction standing on a street corner chatting to people or idly watching life go by. We had no way of gauging his anxiety, or that of others in Kusumpur Pahari, but felt that some good was being done by the familiarities of the street.

The settlement's topology allows the easy circulation of information and formation of shared intelligence. We quickly found clear consensus on Kusumpur Pahari's problems, singling out piped drinking water, jobs and primary education, gender inequality, youth errancy, alcohol and substance dependency, and the threat of eviction. So, too, with the view that the settlement needed better quality municipal services, assurances against eviction, more training and empowerment initiatives, and incentives to motivate the idle and wayward. While this intelligence arises out of common experience, and in the case of individuals such as Aman, Bimal, Gita, Sonia and the Wing Commander from a sense of civic duty, it is also the product of outdoor conversations on the *maidan*, at water tankers, around open fires and card games, in streets and alleyways, on the way home from work and school, outside shops and places of worship and during moments of rest in the evening beyond the threshold. In these conversations, information, opinions and comparisons circulate, their repetitions building shared expertise of adjustments, anticipations and manoeuvres needed to negotiate lack, hardship and uncertainty. The encounters pass on what is known, but importantly, they also deepen and spread ground expertise, both enabled by the intimacies of coproduced public space. The vernacular intelligence does not coalesce as a form of collective agency pressing for particular policy interventions or managing common problems (e.g. the removal of grey water), nor does it provide surety in confronting the adversity, disadvantage and deprivation that slum dwellers face. Instead, it is one more source of experiential knowledge to manage the self in an often opaque and bewildering epistemic environment in which many kinds of knowledge – statal, professional, religious and vernacular – require interpretation (Das, 2022).

Conclusion

To delve into the ecology of neglected places is to uncover states of wellbeing and belonging formed in the practices of negotiating a challenging life in a distinctive habitat, to be alerted to shades of 'vulnerability and politics . . . interwoven in concrete lives' (Han, 2018: 340). In Kusumpur Pahari and Yamuna Pushta, threaded into the shades of wellbeing and attachment are biographies of the self, affordances of space, infrastructures of care and provision and relations with contiguous others, casting doubt over syntheses of community detached from lived experience typified by nativist nationalism despite its claims to know the ground of the left-behind. For such syntheses to become more than rallying cries for or against the left-behind, they must connect with and rework the formations of subjectivity in situated dwelling. The comparisons between Yamuna Pushta, organized care for the homeless and Kusumpur Pahari reveal the combined agency of material circumstances, habitat characteristics, provisioning structures and spaces of care and interaction in shaping life chances and social dispositions. In these comparisons, there has been no intention to imply that all is well in Kusumpur Pahari (or the many other informal settlements like it in Indian cities). The settlement remains a place of inadequate provisions, insecure housing tenure, malfunctioning infrastructures, overcrowded homes, governmental neglect and considerable want and poverty. But in the decadal geography of auto-construction followed by municipal and civic servicing, and in the propinquities of dense cohabitation, its residents have managed to find support and opportunity as well as to build social connections and a strong sense of place. Any similar outcomes for the homeless in Old Delhi have arisen because of the care and effort of NGOs operating permanent housing shelters and recovery centres.

The urgency to find a way from the open camp to the serviced settlement is marked in the present biopolitical moment in India. Covid-19 and responses to it have disproportionately affected the poorest, confined in crowded slums, cleared from camps such as Yamuna Pushta, neglected by clinics, rendered unemployed, shunned in the street as carriers of the disease, only occasionally helped by overstretched charities and citizen groups, but largely left to their own devices to survive. A graphic illustration is the march of the poor over hundreds of miles to their home provinces during lockdowns. Already challenged by multiple precarities, as shown here and by countless other studies, the homeless and slum dwellers have been made ever more disposable by the epidemiology of the pandemic, while the politics of care has tarnished them as dangerous subjects. No matter how loudly the current government proclaims to have the interests of the (Hindu) poor at heart, its acts and ground troops escalate the threats of eviction, the erasure of those without papers to prove their identity under the new citizenship laws, the communalist violence that plays out worst in the slums, and the attacks on Muslims who are nothing less than Indian citizens (Chatterjee, 2023). Policy improvements for the homeless and slumdwellers have tended to come from progressive subnational states and municipal governments as well as from NGOs in the field doing what they can. They have not come from a government whose attempts to draw the poor into a battle against fictive local and national enemies has been far stronger than securing their lives and habitats. Its acts on the ground before and during the pandemic have done little to lift the least well-off above the hollow rhetoric of wresting the nation from elites and middle classes and promises of cultural, ethnic and religious inclusion in its anti-poverty and citizenship programmes.

Fortunately, poor neighbourhoods like Kusumpur Pahari still offer relations of cohabitation able to fend off individual alienation and social animosity. Their habits of collective life contradict nationalist portrayals of life on the margins and of imagined community. The Delhi evidence, developing arguments in the last chapter about urban conviviality, has shown how distinctive vernaculars of social wellbeing and disposition form in the topographies and rhythms of lived space (and, for that matter, in other spaces of routine encounter such as schools, workplaces and associations). It shows how even in the most demanding existential conditions, coproduced places can foster social reciprocity, common knowledge and a shared sense of place through the overlaps of spatial contiguity and relational proximity. Such binds are not symptoms of 'cohesive community', in the sense of strong local ties and obligations, but of place lived and produced together, its frequency of public encounter, common endeavour and shared infrastructure helping to reinforce togetherness in difference. This kind of place offers clues to a national politics of belonging, encouraging it to think about the co-habitability of environments, conditions of social encounter, equities of care and provision and affordances of public space. It proposes imagined nation from the ground of lived interactions, whose virtues of coexistence and common life have nothing to do with the myths of tradition, sovereignty and privileged subjects peddled by the advocates of native nation.

3

The Intimate Public Sphere

Introduction

If the places where people actually live are the neglected sites of belonging in national jousts of imagined community, it is partly because of the digital transformation of the public sphere into an intimate relational space in which battles of national identity and affiliation are fought out. Historically, it has been assumed that democracies with a free and active public sphere stave off authoritarian tendencies because of a plurality of voice and authority, yet today's advances of strongarm nationalism in India, Brazil, Turkey, the UK, Poland, Italy, Hungary and the US are being made in just this kind of public sphere. There is a paradox to be explained in order to account for and address the progress of nativism through the public sphere. There is a prominent tradition of thought that needs to be revisited, its protagonists such as Émile Durkheim, John Dewey, Walter Lippmann, Hannah Arendt, Jürgen Habermas and Chantal Mouffe arguing that the combined force of the free circulation of information and knowledge, an empowered civil society and a public culture of dissent and debate is necessary to keep power in check. It presumes that the society of active citizenship, civic organization, media diversity, free speech and public deliberation can contain demagogic politics through the balances and interactions of representative and participatory democracy. It would locate the escalation of strongarm nationalism in the corrosion of this democratic public sphere, deeming its restoration necessary for an antinationalist politics of belonging. Yet in reality, all but the most authoritarian democracies (whose regimes do indeed control the public sphere) abound with independent civic and political activity and critical commentary from a wide range of media outlets. In turn, citizens participate in numerous online and offline networks of information, opinion and sentiment. They have become consequential publics constantly addressed by political and cultural organizations vying for influence, active participants in agitations for and against demagoguery, racism and liberalism as we have seen in recent years. In this field of many actants and voices circulate diverse interests and intelligences backed by vernacular and scientific expertise, certified and noncertified data, and rational and folk claims. The public sphere has become an epistemic field of multiple regimes of truth and opinion.

The public sphere of the threatened democracies remains plural, populated and participatory, with digital technologies playing their part in the proliferation and expansion of small geographies of social intimacy and affiliation. This is why fringe ideological and political movements have been able to grow, their expanded reach and influence helped rather than hampered by an 'unruliness' that progressives would want regulated so as to restore the public sphere of civic pedagogy and democratic deliberation. It is a moot question whether the untethered public sphere can be reined in along these lines or can prevent fabrications passing as public truths through aggressive online campaigns backed by powerful sponsors, political organizations and media giants. Could it not be that the public sphere has become too vast and unleashed, and paradoxically too intimate, to be rescued as an arena of deliberative democracy and civic formation? In this case, a reparative politics of the public sphere may need to look elsewhere, for example, to rules of conduct to prevent fabrications from escalating, for example, through sanctions against the machinery, money and muscle behind harmful incitement. It may need to find a way of harnessing the expressive freedoms, multiple logics and structures of feeling enabled by digital platforms to common interests, causes and pedagogies of publicness, instead of seeing them as betrayals of the public sphere of rational or agonistic engagement. This is the thrust of thinking in this chapter in recognizing the public sphere as plural, thymotic and polysemic, but also technologically stacked up in favour of powerful sectional and corporate coalitions.

In its contemporary form of many intimate communities, plural rationalities of truth and belief and active jostling for influence, the public sphere has become an important site of belonging. Hosting countless virtual spaces of affiliation and identity formation, lively projections of imagined community and organized manipulations of thought and feeling, it has become much more than a space of interactive expression. It is the battleground of imagined community, certainly the springboard of a nationalist politics of belonging at a pace ahead of progressive efforts to develop a politics of convivial coexistence. The chapter opens with an account of the cultural inflections of the public sphere decided in the plays of civic, technological and political agency. It traces public balances of conviviality and animosity to infrastructural skews and to the machinations of organized interests, further examined in the second section through an analysis of the digital public sphere, which has become the beating heart of social interaction and orientation. Focusing on the liveliness of social media, the section explores tensions between the social freedom to vocalize, algorithmic agencies with their own logics and political economy, background content and private life seamlessly pouring into the public foreground, and the power of the organized players lurking behind digital platforms. The section sets out a case for public service impositions on IT providers, ethical scrutiny of algorithms and stringent antitrust and anti-harm rules as infrastructural basics for a more common and interactive public sphere. The third section, prompted by scepticism of science and expertise that lies at the heart of nativism and its popular success, discusses the making of public truths. Taking encouragement from the return of public trust in professional and evidence-based knowledge during the pandemic, and taking its cue from social studies of science showing public truths as earned and not preordained, it urges progressive acceptance of public knowledge as socially constructed and affectively mobilized instead of relying on restoration of the public primacy of science, reason and expertise in order to disrobe the grammar of nativism. Its premise is that progressive cause for cultural affinity in difference would be better served by approaching the public sphere as a theatre of persuasions by engaging with vernacular and experiential knowledge and accepting that all truths need public validation. This necessitates engaging with the concerns and beliefs of nativist publics, building affective empathy with the worlds of evidence and expertise, and bridging epistemic differences in campaigns of common cause that reinforce publicness as a code of belonging.

Thinking the Public Sphere

The blurs of deliberation and sentiment currently favouring nativist political instincts are well illustrated by four examples of how intimate publics form. In his analysis of Hindu nationalism, Moyukh Chatterjee (2016) has argued that Hindu demands in Gujarat in 2002 for a shutdown (*bandh*) of businesses and offices to condemn the killing of Hindu activists by a Muslim mob, one that unleashed mass violence against innocent Muslims, was more than a top-down political venture. The *bandh*, according to Chatterjee, was a 'form of political drama when crowds perform claims to sovereignty' (p. 294), enabling a Hindu public to think it could take on the role of government to discipline co-citizens of India. In this, the spectacle of the *bandh* as an event proved essential in inviting Hindus from all walks of life and social strata to perform a drama of aggrieved sovereigns feeling entitled to punish Muslims. The *bandh* is one of many theatrical convocations since then, fabricating Hindus as a wronged majority, their demonstrations of rage and righteousness core to nationalist reordering of India as an anti-secular and non-Muslim state.

How an aesthetic of grievance makes counter-publics is well illustrated in Premesh Lalu's (2017) analysis of the 'Trojan Horse' murder during a school boycott in 1985 of three schoolchildren in Cape Town by South African security forces hiding in wooden railway crates. For months black and coloured students in the Eastern Cape had stayed away from school to oppose the state of emergency declared by the apartheid state in July 1985, engaging in protests and pitched battles against the security forces. In explaining the students' courageousness to persist despite the dangers faced, Lalu acknowledges the role of pent-up rage against a system bearing down on every aspect of the lives of the majority population, but he uncovers another important factor. This was the encouragement provided by seeing large numbers of black and coloured peers claim the streets, but also watching films at the local cinema that carried the students to other worlds 'lived inside memory, as a prosthesis of memory of spaces not yet inhabited' (2017: 262). The interplay of shared anger and visual mobilization made and sustained this temporary public.

Writing on the deliberative public sphere considers codes of conduct such as civility to be an important lubricant of respectful dialogue between opposed publics. In his pioneering work on the rise of the bourgeois public sphere, Jürgen Habermas (1991) shows how new codes of urban speech, dress and comportment marked the civic etiquette of an emerging nineteenth-century café culture. A recent example is Aaron Ansell's (2017) analysis of blessings (*bençao*) liberally used in conversations in north-east Brazil to smooth things over and maintain hierarchies of respect and deference. Ansell argues that during the 2000s when a new age of electoral democracy was unfolding in Brazil after the long military dictatorship, in areas such as the rural north-east steeped in traditions of familial, clientelist and patronage politics, blessings as a ritual of deferential civility took on an important role during voting campaigns. The liberal use of blessings by candidates allowed traditional leaders to maintain their old support base as well as to court the 'modern' voter interested in the content of party manifestos, by helping to defuse tensions during often volatile exchanges. An old convention of phatic civility passed into the region's new political environment as a code of public behaviour facilitating respectful dialogue between old and new senses of place, decades later thoroughly torn into by Bolsonaro's vituperative politics.

The fourth example, returning to Gujarat, reveals how charismatic events sustain a public, in this case mixing religious myth and political reasoning. Mona Mehta (2017) writes about the rise of a 'Guru-sphere' in Hindu nationalist politics, illustrated by ticket-only gatherings featuring 'star' religious figures who reinterpret sacred Hindu texts and Gandhian idioms to question India's post-independence commitment to constitutionalism, religious and cultural tolerance, and the secular nation (all of which Gandhi actually defended). Hindutva bonds at these events tighten through mesmerizing stories weaving sacred texts, myths and social commentary, told in the embrace of lush furnishings, fragrant aromas, sacred music and guru charisma emanating the revelatory aura of Hindu nation. An irony is that the events rely on the permissiveness of the Indian constitution to discredit it, the 'tendency to produce hegemonic monologues over pluralistic dialogues' arising 'not in the absence of, but through, the institutional mechanisms of deliberative democracy'. Mehta explains 'these exclusivist practices are enabled and protected by democratic liberal procedures – such as the laws that guarantee the right of assembly, a free press that broadcasts these events, and civic society organisations that orchestrate the gurus' gatherings' (2017: 502).

These are not four examples of dramatic excess in the public sphere of non-Western democracies. They also illustrate the significance of the choreographic, cinematic, phatic and charismatic in the public life of the West. The orchestration of aura is inseparable from the rationalities of deliberation (Habermas, 2007 [1981]), democratic expression (Dewey, 2012 [1927]) or agonistic disagreement (Mouffe, 1999) expected of the liberal public sphere. According to Frederick Dolan (2018), Hannah Arendt (2009 [1963]) understood this well when commenting on the charisma of the American Constitution, by suggesting that popular interest in the American Revolution grew because the narrative tone of the Constitution presented the new American Republic's founding as a myth of beginning, interruption and rebirth, subsequently embellished by popular novels and leaders with the details of the new world. Dolan explains that in contrast to 'America's own understanding of itself as the realization of timeless truths, immutable principles or absolute ideas, Arendt's narrative reveals another America, one adrift in the unpredictable, uncontrollable perlocutionary consequences of its momentous privileging of the discursive' (2018: 199). Popular interest coalesced around the cajolements of a moral tale of destiny, as could a clear and sequential narrative of journey today for progressive opposition to nativism, imbued with an aura of desire and necessity through charismatic staging.

Pivotal in these cultural orientations is the work of intermediaries. The orchestrations of thinktanks, pundits and opinion makers (and the infrastructures and corporations of the media and online industries discussed in the next section) are hardly incidental. They make public culture, as exemplified by Hugo García's (2019) analysis of the machine of public propaganda in the UK between 1914 and 1950, showing how government channels, newspapers, civic associations and renowned figures naturalized public opinion in favour of the war effort or British exceptionalism in Europe. The campaigns oscillated between explicitly manipulating public opinion, appealing to common sense and encouraging free debate, depending on the balance between conservatives and liberals and opinion on the relative merits of propaganda and public instruction. Later, as mass observation polls and other ways of monitoring public opinion became available (showing that Britons valued facts, reliable news and open debate, and bristled at attempts to bend their thinking), subtler forms of public persuasion attuned to survey polls emerged, appealing to 'common sense' and moral argument. García proposes that 'the successive attempts by governments and elites to catch and sway the shifting public mood suggests that [this] had a greater influence in shaping the UK's democracy than has sometimes been assumed' (2019: 395). This is only one illustration of a long history of intermediation in the democracies qualifying the meaning of the liberal public sphere as a space of free civic deliberation.

The growth of intermediaries has eroded distinctions of source and sought opinion. For example, to get close to voters, politicians routinely rely on professional speechwriters to add a human touch and narrative force to their speeches. Jaap de Jong and Bas Andeweg (2011) show how for some time Dutch politicians have abandoned civil servants and political advisers writing dry, factual and elaborate speeches, for media professionals able to craft short talks punctuated by rhetoric, personal anecdotes, case histories and emotional charge. This has been a deliberate move to gain public traction by connecting policy messages to emotional intelligence and professional authority to personal authenticity. Similarly, pundits who now litter the political landscape, have narrowed the gap between political messaging and media independence in the public sphere. They have become staple public commentators, they help politicians and elites to place and tailor their messages, and they smooth relations between parties. Rita Figueiras (2019) shows this in a study of pundits actively managing their stakes in the public arena, helping media organizations to maintain good relations with politicians (and vice versa), and reinforcing the co-dependence of the media and circles of power. She comments 'more than being interested in, or oriented to, informing grass roots audiences or representing the interests or perspectives of civil society, punditry seems to be a field primarily oriented to the pundits themselves and managing power stakes in the public arena' (p. 181). The rise of a 'punditry sphere that revolves around the circles of power' (p. 172), she notes, has closed the gap between politics and marketing, governing and campaigning, and messaging and massaging, reducing public opinion making to 'a one-way communication process' (p. 181). Intermediaries have become the obligatory passing points of political discussion, the crowds of pundits, gurus, lobbyists, think-tanks, propagandists and opinion makers mediating civic and political encounter in the public sphere.

It is in this environment that new civic and political demands have to make their way, looking for manoeuvre in a controlled public sphere, one that is especially restrictive in authoritarian democracies. In their study of civic activism in Singapore and Uganda, for example, Daniel Hammett and Lucy Jackson (2018) show that constrained by strong rules of censure, the activism is channelled by strong state and restrictive precepts of civic participation. Singapore's governmental and public ordinances of 'peace and tranquillity' have produced forms of civic activism restricted to social affairs and actively monitored by the state, 'required to embody civil(ity) as being "respectful" of laws and norms and "peaceful" in activities while contributing to economic development goals and efforts to create racial and social harmony' (p. 149). In Uganda, a civic sphere restricted by legislation, state surveillance and government harassment of social activists has been confined to acts of service delivery and welfare provision, prevented from profane independence as proven by the attacks on the opposition led by Bobi Wine during the 2021 national elections. In both countries, the civic operates under sharp state surveillance.

Civic activism in less restricted public spheres is also a game of manoeuvre based on cultural presumptions of the social contract. This is shown in Lisa Mitchell's (2018) study of public assemblies and mass protests in South India performed as a form of non-adversarial exercise to engage with government by holding officials to electoral promises. Mitchell describes the theatricality of public fasts, workplace walkouts and street occupations in Hyderabad and elsewhere in the state of Telangana as 'roars of the people' to 'hail the state' for policy reforms. Disagreeing with interpretation of such dissent as the insurgency of a rights-seeking 'political society' (Chatterjee, 2011), Mitchell sees in it the tactics of a rights-bearing 'civil society' to secure attention from a state 'that entertains and gives audience to the concerns and grievances of those who are governed, and recognizes them as political subjects' (2018: 223). Mitchell highlights the performative character of civic mobilization, in this example, anticipating victory from tactics that paradoxically reify 'state sovereignty in their appeal to its authority and eager desire for recognition and interpellation into networks of authority' (p. 227). The orchestrations are intended to attract a regional state that otherwise does not engage, something the national government has singularly ignored in its contempt for protests by students, Muslims, women, minorities and secularists against its attacks on civil, religious and liberal freedoms.

These illustrations nudge a counter-politics towards the tactics of manoeuvre in the mediated public sphere rather than towards its restoration as a court of rational deliberation, while accepting Habermas's (2007 [1981]) understanding of pubic reasoning as a pedagogy of citizenship. This is an uncertain pedagogy, though, as research on citizen juries shows. One example is a study by Vincent Jacquet of organized public deliberations in Belgium, discovering that no more than 3 per cent of a canvassed public signed up for a local authority event in 2015 to take citizen soundings on environmental priorities, a 'G1000' event to gather views on social security, immigration and wealth redistribution after the 2011 elections when the country had no government for several months, or a 'G100' event held to test long-term municipal goals in a locality south of Brussels. The study finds that citizens who declined to participate cited as reasons shyness, reticence, diary conflicts or scepticism about the political nature of the events (Jacquet, 2017), while the small minority that agreed to participate did so to meet other people, learn more about the issues discussed or make their voice heard (Jacquet, 2019). Any pedagogy of citizenship was incremental, involving people already 'politically interested, attentive to the news and concerned by some public issues' (Jacquet, 2019: 650), accustomed before participating in the juries to the everyday sociality of living-room talk, garden-fence conversations and casual exchanges with strangers (Schmitt-Beck and Grill, 2020).

Even such a civic pedagogy is not immune from the wider cultural politics of participation shaping social perception of the worth of engagement. This is especially so when the political 'system' is sensed to be corrupt. Natalie Fenton (2018) suggests that liberal democracy itself has become a constraint felt by citizens to serve elite interests, betray political promises and ignore ordinary people, putting them off participating in public life. In the context of a 'post-public' culture of 'volatility, fragmentation and polarization' displacing a recent past of 'relatively extensive, shared and stable public spheres' (Davis, 2019, cited in Schlesinger, 2020: 1553), the disenchantment plays into sectionalist affiliations when citizens decide to participate. It's another kind of civic pedagogy. As William Davies (2021) argues, escalations in the post-public sphere of populist denunciation, neoliberal abandon and digital posturing have eroded conventions of social equivalence enabling claims to be judged through shared meanings and measures of worth. Ever louder congregations against settled political culture feeding off dogged individualism and the hyperactive digital subject have made the public sphere a stage of 'performances within an unending game of attack and counterattack' (p. 53) slowly chipping away at codes, rules, infrastructures of common encounter. This is the context of any (hapless) progressive effort to encourage a pedagogy of civic preparedness from the public sphere.

It is a context of powerful drifts of parallel isolation accelerated by the digital media. In the public sphere of immersive algorithmic worlds with hidden technical and corporate logics, Davies argues that the 'very principles through which social life "holds together" ... are no longer apparent to those who participate ... meaning that "suspicion" is an entirely understandable critical stance' (2021: 60). In virtual participation, evaluations no longer emerge from a priori principles of social judgement but from algorithmic summaries of mass information by actors with the 'extra-juridical' power to process data, treating people not as persons but as cyborgs responding to machine stimuli. Publics take shape performatively around digital attractors such as brands sorting through masses of data to engineer social dispositions and attachments via simple signs such as emojis and memes or the shorthand of online symbols of like and dislike requiring 'minimal semiotic mediation' (p. 55). Collective opinions and sentiments arise from coalitions of human and nonhuman actants turning live and archived digital content into sensible holds on social attention and relying on arts of code-led categorization and visual capture to curate temporary publics.

Digital Unruliness

Accounts of digitally mediated publics see them as echo chambers of opinion and sentiment maintained by catchy symbols, charismatic personalities, myths of authenticity and animated data, sometimes performed live at large physical gatherings through combinations of chant, charm and chat (cf. Airas, 2021, on the tactics of the populist Sweden Democrat Party). They find congregations of excitable subjects held together by algorithm and affect rather than by reason and dialogue, tonally more disposed to emotive political causes such as nativism than to sedate campaigns for pragmatic and democratic advancement. The Trump bubble, for example, persists despite the wild, incoherent and inaccurate utterances of its protagonist because of semiotic associations 'below people's threshold of consciousness' (Slotta, 2019: 401) struck with discourse in right-leaning websites. Its force is sustained by coded language uniting the personal authority of Trump to alternate facts, truths and nativist quests, undisturbed by fact-checks and proofs of inaccuracy and incoherence. Here, and in other digitally animated publics, interactions mimic preformed cultural dispositions despite the varieties of information and opinion circulating online. This is shown by Ivo Furman and Asli Tunç (2020) in their study of Twitter exchanges on the night of the controversial Turkish Constitutional Referendum in April 2017 that proposed sweeping new Presidential powers. Far from helping people to come to a view based on information shared and debated in public, the feverish online exchanges simply reinforced 'ideological uniformity, polarization, and partisan antipathy ... mirroring existing social tensions in Turkey' (p. 311). The exchanges reinforced existing divisions of opinion, keeping discussion 'mostly unidirectional', stripped of 'any meaningful dialogue' (p. 322). The Twitter noise helped to strengthen Erdoğan's bid for absolute power.

Woven into the fabric of the online public sphere is a stark contradiction. On the one hand, its diverse platforms magnify opportunities for individuals to participate in multiple and distant social worlds through a myriad of horizontal relationships. On the other hand, the interactions are not free or direct. As Evan Stewart and Douglas Hartmann (2020) observe, on platforms such as Google, Facebook and Twitter, 'algorithmic filtering influences and in fact changes what people see, how inferential analyses like machine learning draw large conclusions about mass behavior, and therefore, how these platforms and their consumer-driven algorithms nudge changes in social behavior by shaping how conversations occur' (p. 176). In the digital public sphere, collective dispositions form around hidden procedures of 'stratified learning, social sorting, and technological design' (p. 176), which, along with the presence of professional organizations and elites routinely shaping public opinion, necessitate some rethinking of the public sphere. Stewart and Hartmann write that while 'Habermas saw the public sphere as a space of intersubjective communication that has been permeated by market interest, we see the increasingly fractured, pluralistic public sphere as an autonomous, interstitial social field that sits between the market, government, and civic society organizations and produces its own cultural logics' (p. 180).

Such centripetal tendencies are encouraged by software configurations. One study compares 250,000 messages posted on Twitter, Facebook and WhatsApp over a 16-month period related to a controversial killing in Israel in March 2016 (Yarchi et al., 2021). It analyses the heated public discussion that followed the decision by a military court to sentence an

Israeli sergeant for 18 months for killing, instead of arresting, a Palestinian who had attacked another Israeli soldier in Hebron. The sentence was opposed by 51 per cent of the Israeli population and supported by 36 per cent at the time of the conviction. The study finds that even six months into the sergeant's imprisonment, Twitter exchanges remained among the likeminded, hardening stances on the sentence and Facebook's public pages continued stand-offs between opposing camps, while only two WhatsApp political discussion groups saw some respectful interaction and diminution of 'hostility toward discrepant viewpoints' (p. 113). For the authors, the differences were accentuated by 'structural features and affordances offered by different social media environments' (p. 114), clarified by another study as the agency of platform conditions such as 'anonymity, persistence, coordination, automation, visibility, searchability, availability' (Bimber and de Zúñiga, 2020: 705) that platform gatekeepers can adjust. This study finds that oppositional escalations in the public sphere are not divorced from practices by domain controllers and powerful users to obscure sources of information, sustain deceptions of authorship through machine learning and photoshopping, and fabricate public opinions, for example, through bot swarms and other crowd technologies corralling people behind particular agendas. The virtual public sphere of participating millions is no marketplace of ideas and exchanges, but an organized space of untraceable claims requiring little proof and in which independent expertise and authority is unable to exert influence over content and its communication and regulation because of the power of domain controllers and major corporate interests.

This constraint is amplified by the circulation of counterknowledges with their own epistemic rationales. According to Tuuka Ylä-Antilla (2018), for example, right-wing Finnish websites opposing immigration or the climate emergency take care to base their claims in rational argument and counterfactual evidence. Wary of unsubstantiated arguments, they do not appeal to 'common sense' over expertise, as frequently claimed in critiques of populism, but instead set out to show how liberal thinking is biased towards particular values and corporate interests, and how their own findings are rooted in a citizen science backed by alternative facts and epistemic logics. Their focus falls on expanding the field of epistemic reasoning, so as to locate their findings – however far from scientific practice – in a given system of logic, consciously differentiated from prevailing regimes of truth. There are, of course, many other websites and virtual communities that appeal to the wisdom of customary and folk knowledge, but they too follow epistemic logics that need to be understood as such, instead of being dismissed as irrational or archaic. In his survey of right-wing websites united in railing against globalization, immigration, racial, gender and sexual equality, liberal democracy and climate science, Mark Davis (2021) uncovers a shared reliance on conspiracies, unverified facts, disdainful and divisive language and knowledge based on everyday experience to attack liberalism and its protagonists and beneficiaries. He is at pains to argue, however, that once we interpret the public sphere as a field of multiple forms of expertise (see next section), the websites should not be labelled as 'anti-modern, tribal, pre-cosmopolitan', but as 'the very essence of the modern' (p. 156) public sphere of jostling rationalities requiring engagement with popular and customary opinion as a legitimate form of knowhow.

Seeing the public sphere as a battle of epistemic cultures opens the possibility of mobilizing counter-knowledges for democratic ends. Most obviously, the social media have allowed masses, denied access to public and political life, to campaign for recognition, voice and justice. Emblematically, the Arab Spring uprisings of 2011 were sustained by information, tactics and solidarities exchanged online (Castells, 2015). Like more recent pro-democracy campaigns such as those in Hong Kong, the digital interactions did not create 'echo chambers' of polarized sameness, but opened public culture to 'multiple opinions and perspectives' (Lee et al., 2018: 1949) and people from diverse backgrounds. Similarly, causes rehearsed in the social media do not always reinforce closed bubbles of opinion and association, as shown by subaltern groups adopting a democratic vernacular of communication. There are countless examples of inclusive online interaction by marginalized communities to campaign for recognition and a wider politics of social justice. Arvind Kumar Thakur (2020) cites the case of an online campaign in India protesting the suicide of a discriminated Dalit university student, whose social media language helped to build political voice, gather wider public support and expose the hypocrisies of state inclusion policies. Similarly, Dalia Elsheikh and Darren Lilleker (2021) write of tentative steps being taken by women in Egypt to share lifestyle choices and hopes and frustrations in online groups, slowly inserting gendered discussion of personal care, self-esteem and permissiveness into a puritanical and patriarchal public culture.

The digital public sphere, such examples show, hosts a multiplicity of voices, orientations and communities pulling away from commonality. Any generic force in its character as a theatre of plural operations derives from system configurations, suggesting that effort to tackle division and animosity in the public sphere would be better served by altering the sociotechnical properties of the digital ecosystem. One illustration is provided by a study of polarized Twitter discussions in Nepal that led to the expulsion in 2016 of a Canadian software engineer who publicly defended a Human Rights Watch report critical of police violence. Its authors Sohan Sha and Mathieu Quet (2020) observe that the controversy said less about the character of public attitudes on the engineer's act than about the cascades of 'a technology articulated to other technologies' (p. 388), making certain opinions become 'part of the operative machine' (p. 388). They note how the seamless flow of information between three operative environments – the argumentative exchanges on Twitter, the software sorting them into simpler bundles of message, and the state's reassembly of evidence – turned the engineer's careful reading of the Human Rights Watch report into a xenophobic campaign for his expulsion on spurious grounds of visa irregularity. The fault lay in a digital interoperability that allowed conversations to merge across digital domains, enabled governance *by* infrastructure, blurred the lines of distinction between reporting and performing social truths, and dislodged meaning from utterances by incorporating them in a chain of technologically mediated actions.

Such digital interoperability, which has become ubiquitous, has political consequences (in this case turning informed commentary on a widely discussed national topic into condemnation of a foreigner who dared to publicize police violence). It extends the algorithmic agency of software programs, it amplifies the peaks of opinion massaged by computational models and their graphics, and it hybridizes human behaviour. Interconnected machine intelligence has fundamentally altered the making of authority and transmission of meaning in the public sphere by dislodging human-to-human interactions. Louise Amoore (2020) shows this in her study of algorithms in self-programming neural nets developed by business and government to assess security risks, which adapt constantly through 'dialogue' with each other and expand their power in conditions of epistemic contingency and doubt. The algorithms are interactively immersed in society, politics and culture, and their adaptive intelligence far exceeds the task of following source code instructions. Amoore concludes that machine learning has decentred the liberal subject by making social intelligence an 'amalgam of humans and algorithms' (p. 150) working in concert, with 'the doubts of human and non-human beings dwell[ing] together, opening onto an undecidable future' (p. 149). Operative ambiguity of this kind conceals the nature of intelligence behind outcomes of the sort described by Sha and Quet. It nudges a reforming politics of the public sphere to expose, scrutinize and recalibrate the configuration of algorithmic neural networks (see below).

Algorithmic intelligence is altering the rules of social aggregation in the public sphere. As Raymond Lee (2017) argues, online group affinities do not arise from crowds gathering around shared interests, but as swarms of contagious behaviour spurred by technologies of 'the digital superpublic' (p. 90). He cites as an example the growth of online selfie groups, which he sees only partly prompted by the offer of free self-publicity in the digital marketplace, but largely by digital pairing devices such as memes pairing similar faces online and so soliciting swarms of submissions. This superpublic is guided by an 'immanence' of digital aggregation, not by 'collectivity from individual participation' (p. 91), the common patterns of behaviour prompted by algorithmic scans of epiphenomena, typified by smartphone users in busy queues and on packed street crossings immersed in their own virtual worlds but also effortlessly moving with the rhythm of the crowd in physical space. In the new public sphere, it is a 'cohesion of appearances' produced by 'informational contagion' (Lee, 2016: 115) that 'attracts and disseminates certain attitudes, emotions and states of understanding via verbal and non-verbal interaction' (p. 110). Common behaviour is no longer the product of shared experience and direct interactions but of software-facilitated contagions working to the discretions of software sorting.

The result is the remaking of public subjectivity, including digital instantaneity gnawing away, according to Paul Virilio (2012), at the human capacity for philosophical reflection, argument and deliberation that takes time to form in the lived experience of existential struggle and deliberation. Jeff Noonan (2019) sees this kind of accelerated virtual life rubbing against the rhythms of humans as 'beings of the flesh, needy, vulnerable, rooted to definite material contexts, interdependent with each other and capable of governing our collective and individual lives according to universally life-enabling values' (p. 775). Perhaps Noonan overstates the displacement of reflections born from the life led, but not the tendency of online reflexes of distraction and impulsiveness to play into a politics of captive attention in the public sphere. Mitchell Dean (2017) writes of 'the indiscriminate accumulation of acclamation' (p. 425) by icons on social media sites obsessively inviting people to post judgements of 'liking', 'friending' or 'following', reinforcing the restless contemporary ritual of public mood-making through 'algorithmic governmentality' (p. 428). This ritual provides influencers with a mass of surface group information to manipulate and recirculate as authentic public feelings that society begins to take as given. One consequence is the politics of public feelings and imagined community tuning in closely to the sequences of instantaneity, working against parties unable to stay close to the impulsive acclamations and distractions that populist movements thrive on.

This impulsiveness can be validated by easy information from the digital archive. Based on Goffman's (2007 [1959]) distinction between actions in the 'back region' of privacy and those in the 'front region' that others can see, John Thompson (2020) argues that online technologies now allow content from back regions to constantly leak into front regions, such that 'individuals, actions and events are now visible in ways that they simply were not visible in the past, and anyone equipped with a smartphone has the capacity to make things visible to hundreds and even millions of others' (pp. 19–20). For Thompson, such porosity profoundly alters the character of the public sphere by blurring distinctions between the private and public, presenting new material and actors disrupting the authority of traditional gatekeepers such as experts and media professionals, expecting influencers to maintain informational acuity and charisma, and normalizing political instability as leaks, revelations and scandals pour in from the back regions. In this public sphere, crucial for political survival and influence is the cultivation of affective and symbolic power, of the aura and not the content of trust and authority, so as to ride contradictions and anomalies exposed by material from the back regions. Populism, with its focus on aura, charisma and the symbolic, has intuited this necessity far better than its political rivals, relying on extreme stage theatrics in countries such as the UK, India, Brazil, Poland, Hungary, Italy and the US to fend off embarrassments, inconsistencies and exposures unearthed by digital scouring that manage to sink political causes investing in rational argument, factual accuracy and moral integrity.

Nativism thrives on the politics of attention, working the overflows of the digital public sphere and its propensities of mimicry, instantaneity and distraction to make its imagined community and its authentic culture. These proclivities will not disappear and could become the harnesses of progressive opposition, less to affirm the latter propensities than to rework them through opposite digital overflows, aggregations and resemblances making the aura of the common and inclusive nation. The activist politics of gender, sexual, racial and climate justice makes good use of these proclivities across different geographies of struggle, which could be expanded to integrate these struggles and those of class justice into rehearsals in the digital public sphere of the imagined community united in diversity. Such a counter-culture reworking code-facilitated structures of feeling cannot have the terms of digital interoperability stacked against it. Justifiably, thinking on online harm and division playing into the hands of nativism has focused on controlling IT platforms and corporations allowing hateful speech to spread, dark and demagogic forces to organize, untruths and fake news to circulate, and online data to be exploited by commercial and security interests. Dominating the communications landscape, the interests of the major IT corporations far exceed any original public utility function, their profits dependent on unregulated excesses, including the mobilizations of disunity and harm. This is why critics such as Dan Schiller (2020) insist on the return of public service roles through a series of pincer actions including improved public education on the role of telecommunications providers, campaigns to ensure that investigative tribunals foreground the public interest, legal prohibitions against revolving-door appointments and corporate lobbying, and legislation that locks the IT corporations into a public utility network that includes non-profit providers, scrutinizes algorithms on grounds of public service and replaces advertising revenue with government funding for essential services. Central to these reforms is not the break-up of the IT giants, but their subjugation to the logic of public service.

Whether the IT giants can be brought into line in this way remains an open question given the power they wield over states, markets and populations across the globe, routinely mobilized to protect their influence and profits. One opening anticipated in Schiller's reference to algorithmic transparency lies in legislating an ethics of software. Niva Elkin-Koren (2020) proposes the introduction of 'adversarial' algorithms incorporating ethical values into machine learning systems, as part of a 'law by design' nudge of software systems towards public ends, automatically picking out online content tied to private business interests and opaque codes allowing illegal, inflammatory and harmful material. In this way, IT platforms would automatically run content past code incorporating the public interest, testing whether 'decisions contravene ... social interests, such as fair use of free speech' (p. 9). There are other possibilities. Linnet Taylor (2020), responding to Louise Amoore's (2019) plea for more 'post-Cartesian doubt' to address existential risk at a time when algorithms have become a primary mode of evaluation, suggests the routine code-based differentiation of data processed by automated systems by categories of social vulnerability. Noting the absence of socially granular data during the Covid pandemic, she proposes an informatics of automatic scans of 'data on who are, or who become, invisible to official data selection under conditions of duress', suggesting 'migrant workers, the undocumented, the elderly in care homes, and their families being some of those in the case of Covid-19' (p. 2). Accordingly, data collection and analysis would shift from 'the notion of the majority to that of the collective' by presenting, always profiling 'people and groups rather than populations' (p. 5).

Public Truths and Trust in Expertise

Such regulatory moves would still leave intact the plural cultural logics of the public sphere supporting divergent understandings of truth and expertise that nativism has been able to exploit to its advantage. Digital openings have made the public sphere a field of multiple rationalities orchestrated as truths, upending settled hierarchies of epistemic authenticity. Suspicion of science and expertise and liking for the made-up have grown because of the copresence of cultural logics validating different types of knowledge in an evaluative arena of plural measures of worth. The formal and vernacular, experiential and received, rational and intuitive have become equivalents, requiring knowledge authorities old and new to popularize their reasoning and adjust to an oscillating politics of truth that can lean towards science and expertise when life is threatened as during the pandemic, or towards popular vernacular when culture and sovereignty are felt to be at risk. In this public sphere, knowledge differences are amplified by echo chamber dynamics pulling away from settled wisdoms of true and false knowledge, good and bad truth, valid and invalid reasoning. Presumptions of the higher worth of science over folk wisdom or of validated evidence over gut feeling no longer hold. In this public sphere of epistemic cultures able to unfold past each other and settle through hidden technical intelligences and agencies, authority and influence no longer rest on assertions of the worth of one culture over another, such as the superiority and reliability of evidence-based and professional knowledge over other forms of expertise. Assertions abound in criticism of the falsity of nativist claims, but with little political traction in the public sphere of multiple epistemic vernaculars and senses of authenticity. This section thus argues that progressive opposition to nativism has to focus on winning an affective war of words, following insight in social studies of science of knowledge as socially constructed and trusted by the measure of effort put into its public validation. It sees trust in the public sphere for progressive ideas arising not from exposures of the inauthenticity of fake truths and false reasoning but from work on embedding them in a narrative of national promise, aligning diverse interests and intermediaries, and generating an affective aura around them.

There exists ground for these steps in the making of public truths. Surveys of public opinion in populist moments show that the suspicion of trust in science and expertise may be less severe and more nuanced than assumed. One example is a survey by the Institute for Government in 2016 showing that despite fierce public derision of expertise by the Brexit camp during the EU referendum, over four-fifths of the British population consulted wanted politicians to base their decisions on objective evidence and the evidence of professionals and experts. According to Leighton Andrews (2017), this remains standard practice in many areas of government, based on his own ministerial experience in the Welsh Assembly. But he clarifies that politicians faced with multiple demands and time pressures gravitate towards experts with good communication skills able to cultivate the trust of politicians, offer focused advice and appreciate the political and media constraints facing decision makers. Expertise has to hone its skills of communication and persuasion to be taken seriously. Another study by Eri Bertsou and Daniele Caramani (2021) also confirms public endorsement of expertise across a set of European countries differentially challenged by nativism, citing a 2017 survey of preferences for populist, elected-party and technocratic politics in Germany, Ireland, the Netherlands, Sweden, Greece, France, the UK, Poland and Romania. The survey found that even in the last five of these countries experiencing considerable nativist surge, there was support for policy decisions relying on technical expertise. Over half the total population surveyed, including supporters of populist politics, approved of decisions made by experts not 'playing with politics', and even in countries such as Greece, Romania, Poland and Italy weary of party politics, 14–20 per cent of the respondents expressed a preference for technocratic government. Bertsou and Caramani conclude that across divides of party, populist and technocratic politics, prevail 'beliefs around the superiority of skillful, knowledgeable, and scientific experts over politicians' (p. 20).

Other European surveys endorse this preference. Katherine Dommett and Warren Pearce (2019) cite Eurobarometer and UK surveys since the early 2000s of public attitudes towards scientific expertise and citizen influence in policy making, consistently revealing more than 75 per cent support for expert-led policy making and only modest interest in citizen participation. This appears to be especially marked in policy areas thought to be complex or major, as Daniel Maliniak, Eric Parajon and Ryan Powers (2021) show in a study of the landmark Paris Climate Agreement that reveals overwhelming public support for specialists such as climate scientists despite sophisticated and expensive campaigning from the climate denial industry. Importantly, such findings suggest that public backing of nativist mockery of expertise may arise from doubts of trustworthiness, as long argued by Onora O'Neill (2002,

2018), rather than from doubts of trust. In this subtle noun change, the focus falls on the performative practices of experts and their science, as Silvia Camporesi, Maria Vaccarella and Mark Davis (2017) show in a study of how ethical and communicative practice makes for public confidence in sensitive biomedical fields such as genome editing. The authors write of the significance of experts engaging in public dialogue, attending to narrative practices, making themselves understood and addressing the 'ethics, social relations, and meanings of trustworthiness' (p. 29). They link trust to the public performances of expertise.

In this example, public truths are located in 'civic epistemologies' (Jasanoff, 2011) of alignment between experts, authorities, opinion makers and publics, shifting progressive response to nativist vernaculars in the direction of a politics of persuasion. Interestingly, ALLEA, the federation of European Academies of Sciences and Humanities, proposes that science should respond to the proliferation of spurious truths by incorporating into its own principles of self-critical inquiry a 'moral economy that enhances trust' through responsive and honest public dialogue (ALLEA, 2018: 7). This includes elucidating the values, assumptions and interpretive choices behind publicly presented evidence instead of claiming impartial objectivity (especially when addressing controversial knowledge challenges whose truths are far from self-evident). The cost of failing to do this is well illustrated by Claire Norton and Mark Donnelly (2016) in their study of the damage done to public trust in expertise by histories of the Israel-Palestine conflict that present oral and archival material as though it was unambiguous and uncontested. Similarly, an analysis of expert reports regularly commissioned by the Norwegian government to help design policies on important societal challenges, finds that their public trustworthiness would increase if they were to disclose epistemic disagreements and anomalies encountered during the inquiry (Holst and Molander, 2018).

The study, commenting on how expert bias, siloed thinking, political naivety, cognitive error and translational difficulty can creep into an inquiry, suggests that more open discussion in reports of methodological and interpretive ambiguities would strengthen their impact by treating readers as interlocutors.

The assumption here is that when public truths are taken as given, detached from the methods of their genesis, conflicts between experts and their critics can escalate as a war of truth and falsity. By implication, the case of science and reason would be strengthened by disclosure of the premises of evidence converting to social fact. Sheila Jasanoff and Hilton Simmet (2017) suggest that 'to restore truth to its rightful place in a democracy, governments should be held accountable for explaining who generated public facts, in response to which sets of concerns, and with what opportunities for deliberation and closure' (p. 751). Other parties similarly generating social truths could clarify how the givens of claim have arisen, reinforcing in the process a scrutinizing public culture interested in knowing the basis of unsubstantiated truth claims and well-evidenced ones behind which, however, lurk particular categories and moves to work the '*feeling* of facts' (Kelly and McGoey, 2018: 9, emphasis in original). Then, argue Ann Kelly and Linsey McGoey, public discussion of new policy truths generated in fields as diverse as microfinance, corporate philanthropy, social inequality and infectious disease would expect to know more about normative and interpretive premises. It is in a culture of public discomfort with unexplained truth claims that science and expertise stand a better chance of winning public trust, making citizens allies in progressive efforts to disarm the proclamations of nativism.

Social studies of science have long maintained that the translation of knowledge into truth rests on practices in the science of sociotechnical alignment, boundary work, network cultivation and narrative construction (Latour, 2007). This is shown by the degree to which public trust in science in the early months of the pandemic was strengthened by the presence of a 'strong institutional machinery of expertise for data production and dissemination' (Lidskog and Standring, 2020: 443). A network including the World Health Organization, national expert bodies, research institutes, emergency services, forecasting centres, local and central government and health care infrastructures quickly consolidated as a 'social machine' of credible intelligence and social trust in a situation of extreme danger and uncertainty. In the same way, as Alejandro Esguerra (2019) argues, social feel for distant scenarios often rests on 'future objects' such as anticipatory technologies offering climate projections from past trends, foresight exercises portraying different environmental scenarios, and experimental prototypes and simulations of feasible life; all important means of making publics 'feel' for possible existential futures. Future objects give tangible feel to the likely unknown, their science of visualized probabilities allowing expertise, affect and politics to be joined in anticipatory mobilization.

Turning to boundary work, in a study of high-level policy experts, James Palmer, Susan Owens and Robert Doubleday (2019) write of 'locally-situated, material conditions of advice giving' (p. 244) that smooth policy influence through studied interactions between experts, policymakers and politicians. Taking evidence from past Chief Scientific Advisors to the UK government, the study shows how policy success is closely connected to the experts' negotiating skills and reputations, their grounded and diplomatic presentation of evidence, their ability to link research findings to political sensitivities and public beliefs, and their attention to brokering consensus across a range of interests. In locating the passage of contextual truths into an agreed perspective through skills of boundary management, the study eschews linear presumptions of science translating into policy practice once its case is made intelligible. The stakes of boundary work can be high, as Federico Brandmayr (2021) pointedly shows in his account of why six earth scientists were found guilty of manslaughter for failing to recommend evacuation before the L'Aquila earthquake in Italy in 2009 that destroyed the medieval city's historic centre and killed over 300 people. Dissenting with the widely held view that this was a cruel and unwarranted judgment against forecasting failure, Brandmayr argues that on the evening before the earthquake when the geologists met as municipal advisers with a public official to discuss the threat, they did not fulfil a civic rather than scientific duty to recommend evacuation on grounds of public risk aversion and protection. According to Brandmayr, the courts did not rule against scientific error, but against the geologists' failure to reconcile their scientific and civic obligations, that is, to enact their boundary role. Fortunately for them, the scientists were acquitted by the Supreme Court in 2014 after a lengthy legal battle.

The political implication of translational thinking is that science – and expertise in general – have to look beyond their professional rituals to secure public and policy traction. They must enter the public arena with worldly pragmatism. Isabel Stengers (2015b), reflecting on the knowledge politics of climate change and of genetically modified organisms, draws the distinction between science preserving the status quo, sometimes 'complicit in state-making and profit-taking' (Beuret, 2017: 262), and joining in 'common practice' with others including non-experts to build shared knowledge and collective agency over difficult policy matters. In pursuing the latter, science drops any pretence of neutrality and innocence, endeavours to communicate technical steps, refuses the depoliticization of problems, and risks to work with others. While defending the integrity of their methods and standards, science and expertise enter the public arena with charisma, diplomacy and tact, knowing how to make their case, when to give ground and where to forge alliances. A science of common practice cultivates narrative style, like literary writing engaging aesthetically with controversial research (Radin, 2019), such as Michael Crichton's (2005) novel *State of Fear*, vaunted by neoconservatives and climate sceptics for preying on the uncertainties of climate science, and the bestseller *Merchants of Death* written by scientists Naomi Oreskes and Erik Conway (2010) with forensic acuity and literary imagination to expose the tobacco industry.

Such crossings are common in problem-driven science, as illustrated by Christy Spackman's (2020) study of the olfactory coming to help scientists tackling the accidental spillage in 2014 of the industrial solvent Crude 4-methylcyclohexanemethanol (MCHM) into the water system of Charleston in West Virginia. Established scientific tests a few days after the spillage were unable to trace the chemical in its most diluted form, which led the municipality to declare the water safe for domestic use, even though residents complained of a liquorice-like smell in their water. This conundrum prompted the scientists to request daily smell reports from residents, which they incorporated into advice given to the municipality on when water would be *sensed* as safe to drink. The water analysts adapted their methods, convincing politicians initially sceptical of 'citizen science' to heed the sensorial knowledge of residents. In problem-driven science, experimental adaptation is a common practice, as are truths based on the alignment of interests. In a study of mosquito science, Ann Kelly and Javier Lezaun (2017) discover how much effort scientists make to arrange field observatories for 'mutual accommodations between observer and observed, captor and captive, and host and vector' (p. 368) so as to facilitate a 'place-bound form of scientific attention to the patterns and peculiarities of mosquito life' (p. 369). The authors show that a field in which 'investigations unfold against a background of limitless ignorance', the 'production of salience is crucial for entomologists', enabled by laboratory arrangements 'within a habitable geometry [where] objects and figures strike the viewer and command her or his attention' (p. 389). Improved public awareness of the worldly practices of science – ultimately the responsibility of its advocates – would greatly improve the profile of professional expertise as citizens and critics begin to appreciate the pragmatic crafts of piecing together knowledge without any compromise of rigour and integrity.

The task here is to invoke and encourage expertise as common practice, as collaborative knowhow in translation. It should be known, for example, that in the aftermath of Hurricane Katrina, when government response to the destruction in New Orleans was slow and disinterested in the poor, communities came together to rebuild neighbourhoods, often in collaboration with university researchers to develop imaginative housing, recreation and arts projects, and validate grassroot knowhow in university outreach programmes (cf. Koritz and Sanchez, 2009). It should be known that disparate groups opposed to the controversial Keystone XL and Dakota Access pipelines supported by the Trump administration mounted a successful case against the powerful state and oil industry lobby by learning to expertly present customary, symbolic and historical objections to the project's environmental impact as legitimate evidence in an inquiry with strict rules of engagement (Bosworth, 2019) by exposing the mendacity of the lobby's efforts to tarnish the opposition. Public assurance would grow from consultative expertise formed in joint endeavour, as shown in Karen Hébert's (2016) study of a public consultation exercise to evaluate the risk to salmon fishing posed by a proposed metals mine in Bristol Bay, Alaska. Hébert argues that although the inquiry favoured interests better versed in technical, scientific and deliberative reasoning, the opposition diplomatically brought together 'multiple forms of knowledge and authority in the public view' (p. 108) around a case for the 'unknown common' and forced the inquiry to broaden its consideration of possible outcomes. The collaborations generated an 'associative expertise' (Moore, 2021) with its own temporality of risk assessment that the inquiry had to take into account.

A knowledge politics of common interest could work with customary knowhow to get past dichotomies of expert and lay intelligence and bring folk wisdoms into dialogue with scientific knowledge. It could recognize the knowhow of lived experience and embodied response to epistemic uncertainty and overload as a form of popular trust in shared culture. Illustratively, James Slotta (2017) writes of arts of listening in parts of Papua New Guinea that have evolved as a way of diplomatically sifting through insincere or deceptive talk without the help of authoritative superiors. Similarly, Lili Lai and Judith Farquhar (2020) write of the 'embodied and emergent ways of knowing' (p. 412) of mountain-herb healers in China who rely on a history of knowledge of medicinal herbs and close examination of a patient's health history and symptoms to gather particular herbs at particular times to offer bespoke treatment. They identify an art of cultivated knowledge of plant, soil and climate properties as well as of the whole lived life, requiring iterations between different types of diagnostic expertise eschewing matched formulas of symptom and cure. It is 'second nature' expertise, a term Steven Shapin (2019) uses to describe the practice in early modern European medicine to label ailments such as phlegm as 'moist' and 'cold' and black bile as 'cold' and 'dry', then matched by doctors to similarly labelled foods considered to cause or cure the ailments. A contemporary example Shapin cites is the lifelong management of illnesses such as diabetes or cardiovascular disease based on 'expert advice on what body-changing habits one ought to reject, maintain, or modify' (p. 26). Progressive harnesses of common understanding in the public sphere could work with second nature expertise, curious to know that in war-torn South Sudan, Western diagnosis of the new nation as an example of governance failure remains ignorant of how community leaders resolve grievances through ethical conciliations and pragmatic diplomacies (Kindersley, 2019), and that aspiring urbanites in Russia still draw on communist pedagogy on the bourgeois family, work–life balance and sexual freedom to negotiate their post-socialist ethical dilemmas of love, leisure and desire (Kruglova, 2017). Second nature knowledge carries tradition meaningfully into the present, expecting a politics of public trust in expertise to acknowledge it.

In sum, work on enacted expertise – professional and didactic or customary and experiential – locates public truths in the alignment of the second nature and the professional. It encourages a progressive politics of belonging in the public sphere to recognize the 'value of conversations' across epistemic boundaries (Walker, 2020: 1), to acknowledge knowledge formed in lived experience and bodily awareness (cf. Voronka, 2016, on how the mentally ill and their professional carers generate new awareness), and to encourage collaborative learning (cf. Withers, 2020, on how feminist classes in the 1960s and 1970s enabled deskilled and gender-stereotyped women to learn new skills through joint craftwork). It can be described as a politics of truth open to epistemic disturbance in the encounter, interested in mothers in Mexico confronting obfuscating official truths by organizing their own inquiries to trace the fate of their 'disappeared' children (Cruz-Santiago, 2020), in sonic testimony such as the recorded breathlessness of a suffocating man used by the family of a native Australian killed by a prison guard to confront written judicial evidence (de Souza, 2020), and in sensorial counter-knowledge, such as the wail of people, car horns and banging pots in the streets of Kathmandu to oppose judicial complacency towards violence against women in Nepal (Kunreuther, 2018). These are just some among many examples of a public epistemology of border transgression.

Conclusion: In the Public Interest

Truths in today's animated public sphere settle because of the machinery of validation behind them. Digital expansions have enabled multiple epistemologies to coexist without cross-reference, throwing established conventions of authenticity to the wind, typified by divided opinion on whether leaving the EU would damage the British economy and whether masks would contain the Covid-19 virus. Public truths turn out to be situated, contested and culturally inflected, their authority nested in wider structures of feeling, and carried by infrastructures of persuasion that are never only technical. Expertise has to pass muster through embedded interests and worldviews, and through the interpretive filters of trusted networks of attachment. The public reception of truth and expertise does not depend on the social status of particular forms of knowledge or the degree of social trust in professional opinion, but on its ability to anticipate opposition, make alliances, straddle boundaries, prove its necessity and create affective momentum. The theatricality of the public sphere presents experts and their advocates with the challenge of mastering the arts of enrolment and nesting truths within customary vernaculars of meaning. The purveyors of folk truths offering no evidence of proof have intuited this with some public success. For progressive politics to make way in this public sphere, it has to win a war of words and emotions by investing its truths with coalitional force, affective energy and customary legitimacy. Its reasoning for the cohabited open nation will make sense to publics drawn to nativism only through labours of persuasion addressing the dilemmas of plural and shifting epistemic culture covered in this chapter.

For traction, these labours, still facing a restless war of manoeuvres with few guarantees in the public sphere, will require altered platform architectures currently controlled by code script, machine learning and powerful organized interests. If the public sphere has become more open and participatory, the biases of code amplified by machine-to-machine communication, and the manoeuvres of IT, media and commercial corporations, as well as charismatic movements and personalities, impede its operation as a pluriverse in which direction arises from free interaction. This is why, as argued in the section on the digital public sphere, a common interest politics must press for ethical indexation of platform arrangements (e.g. their algorithms, commercial interests and harmful content), stronger anti-trust legislation to break up the power of IT and media corporations and orient them to a public service function, and stringent controls on false, inflammatory and harmful activity. It must seek to simultaneously change platform configurations and tackle the corporate and demagogic interests profiting from the status quo.

In parallel, the pursuit of the common in the polyvocal public sphere would benefit from explicit progressive advocacy for a pedagogy of collaborative intelligence on pressing societal and epistemic challenges. This would reinforce the public sphere as a space of collective inquiry and shared intelligence, wary of uncorroborated knowledge and unexplained received wisdom, and expecting opinion-makers and authorities to work for the public interest. Then, conversations across the garden fence and in public spaces, at social gatherings and campaigns, in schools and workplaces and in the digital and nondigital media might begin to call out interests gaining from public fragmentation, indifference and ignorance. In his reflection on how globalists fixing on new worlds and localists fixing on old places could find common ground, Bruno Latour suggests that a public pedagogy of 'earthliness' (2018) and 'critical zones' (Latour and Lenton, 2019) might nudge disagreeing parties towards joint address of the severe existential risks posed to everyone everywhere by the climate emergency. In making shared habitability the common goal, the prevalent anthropocentric humanism fighting for globalism or localism would start to give way, as

Dipesh Chakrabarty (2019) suggests, to a planetary humanism that places the future of the habitable earth at the centre of concern. Thus reinforced, the dialogues of the public sphere might turn towards seeing the common injuries and common strengths of national and planetary survival.

The language of #MeToo and Black Lives Matter has begun to work in this way, crossing the lines of gender, race, class and nation in common dissent against multiple forms of injustice. Henry Farrell and Hahrie Han (2020) argue that in North America and the UK, the Black Lives movement increasingly links exasperation with a history of racialized wrongs with struggle against other social injustices of an exclusionary and unequal neoliberal order. The movement is becoming an emblem of shared suffering and active remembrance of intersectional violence. It could be commemorated in this way, rather like the Kigali Genocide Memorial Centre remembering the murder of hundreds of thousands of Tutsis during the Rwandan Civil War in 1994, and now a site of public atonement with ample reminders of the oneness of a people and the inhumanity of difference turned into cold murder (Sodaro, 2018). A pedagogy of commonality in the public sphere could also make more of experiments anticipating new ways of common existence. One example is the Occupy movement, which Bill Brown (2020) describes as demonstrably rejecting a culture of isolated, private and hierarchical living by placing communal and democratic living in full view at the heart of privatized and policed public space. Such cohabitation, like the evidence in the chapter on Delhi, makes public a tradition of 'fugitive' life based on subaltern intimacy and spatial sociability, fostering habits of reciprocal listening and learning to survive risk and hostility (Moten, 2018). It identifies expansive alternatives to nativism's secessionist fugitivity.

The ideas presented in this chapter recover an expectation of publicness rather than deliberative dialogue from the history of thought on the public sphere (Ekström, 2021). They reinforce the 'affirmative biopolitics' envisaged by Roberto Esposito (2019) to resist corruptions of democracy produced by media exuberance, politics becoming ever more theatrical and sovereignty turning into the government of bodies. A political aesthetic of publicness making visible myriad practices of care and fellowship in hard times can show that 'within our horizon – the one defined by the irreversible centrality of individual and collective life – a new political subjectivity, as well as a new principle, open and relational, of identity is being reconstructed' (Esposito, 2019: 322). The public sphere can become the space of futurity based on practices of cohabitation, collaboration over common concerns, mobilization of folk and scientific wisdoms and joint curation of the ecologies of the possible (Conley, 2016).

4

Aesthetics of Nation

Introduction

It seems appropriate to end a book on belonging with a chapter on the aesthetics of nation, after the seminal work of Benedict Anderson, Ernest Gellner, Anthony Smith and Mark Billig on the affective power of homeland myths and traditions. Their influence has revealed the intimate ways in which iconic objects and projects, myths and memorials, stories and dramas, and films and songs have shaped meanings and sentiments of nation and national belonging, as well as counterprojects of community. It has shown how the battles of territorial demarcation, citizenship and identity are played out in the frames of imagined community, in intensely felt iconoclastic clashes working the infolds of collective and subjective sentiments of home and the world (Goswami, 2020). Writing on imagined community has shown why fictions of nation have turned out to be politically consequential (cf. Chlup, 2021, on how celebrated texts of sacrifice and defeat have sustained modern Czech nationalism), along with state-endorsed forms of art, architecture and music (Brincker and Leoussi, 2018) and everyday domestic rituals making publics see and feel the call of nation (Duchesne, 2018; Storm, 2017). It has brought into view an aesthetic politics of nation – the ways in which polity and society meld through commonplaces of national authenticity worked deep into the popular imagination. Writing on political aesthetics has revealed the affective power of an industry of state and counter-state symbolic projects, for example national dress or food campaigns typified by nineteenth-century attempts to define 'Dutchness' through the details of dress etiquette (Dellmann, 2018), or resurrections in Slovenia after 1989 of the Kranjska sausage as a national symbol of a 'free' post-socialist nation (Mlekuž, 2020). So, too, political investment in cultural myths of homeland origins and indigenous purity, ranging from indigeneity campaigns in earlier periods of Latin American nation building (Gutierrez, 2018) to contemporary nativist mobilizations against the open society in the Americas, Europe and Asia. The literature explains why the battle over iconic art matters, in revealing the pivotal place of films such as *Birth of a Nation* in popularizing the American myth of white origin cleansed of a history of indigenous genocide and Black slavery (Boyce and Chunnu, 2020), or of agitations of religious community in sixteenth-century Flanders to destroy Catholic imagery and those in this century by ISIS and the Taliban against non-Islamic monuments in Afghanistan (Spicer, 2017). It reveals how affinities between leaders and citizens arise from casual politicking across ludic technologies, such as playful interactions through Obama's election app and Trump's frog meme with millions of American voters (Gekker, 2019). Other writing in this genre finds popular legitimation for national exploits arising from the consumption of charismatic works of scientific, travel or religious revelation (cf. Caraccioli, 2021, on the manipulation by the Spanish Crown for colonial expansion of reports of naturalists travelling to the New World, and Cohn, 2020, on contemporary political causes legitimated through science fiction and fantasy).

In these aesthetic mobilizations is serviced the contract between the governed and governing through popular enactments of political fantasies. They are crucial for the politics of nation moored in sensory distillations of mission and truth, amply evident in contemporary nativist attempts to dislodge the distillations of cosmopolitan nation through a drama of slogans, memes, fictions and narratives consistently outweighing the affective ploys of the opposition. Accordingly, this chapter considers aesthetic options for the politics of cohabitation laid out in the book. It turns to a 'minor' aesthetics amplifying public feeling for generative and collaborative ways of surviving the risks, fragilities and animosities that characterize our times. It proposes arts focusing on the pressure points for common existence and cohabitation, witnessing forms of compassionate susceptibility defying the aesthetics of separation and aversion, and identifying shared atmospheres, places and infrastructures without which even the desire to protect self and same evaporates. The chapter, in its first half, acknowledges the mass force of a 'major' aesthetics of imagined community nested in sensory regimes of rebarbative or romantic nationalism and civic patriotism. While recognizing that the aesthetics of coexistence proposed in the second half of the chapter lacks the panoptic might of these regimes, the case rests on hope in mounting public affection for myriad practices of convivial and common coexistence made visible and desirable as the staples of imagined community, but also on doubt in the ability of an aesthetics of romantic nationalism or civic patriotism to match a rebarbative politics working the viscera of resentment at a time of deep existential insecurity. At most, the chapter finds some affinity between the minor arts set out and the aesthetics of civic nation.

Romantic and Civic Nationalism

The aesthetics of imagined nation has lain at the heart of state-building and regime-toppling projects, working the grain of popular sentiments of the ideal community, its rightful members and its unwanted enemies. It is a history of performance through the details of territorial and cultural demarcation of distinct visions of community eventually taken for granted. Mastering the means and messages of political imagery has been key for state and oppositional movements in bridging coercion and consensus, naturalizing the performances of community and waging war against the old and anomalous. It has been central in battles of position between hegemons and subalterns, as Gramsci showed in elaborating the cultural fault lines of the clashes of capitalism, socialism and fascism in early twentieth-century Italy, and it remains a neglected dimension in Foucault's seminal thinking on how the disciplinary modes of modernity became the lived measures and categories of social life. Starting with utopian imagery that has faded in the twenty-first century but exemplifies the aesthetics of appeal to a future without precedence, this section compares the promise of three sensory regimes projecting the future as return: romantic and rebarbative nationalism and, to a lesser degree, civic patriotism. It notes the irony of invoking a simpler and safer national past in turbulent times while, in the case of rebarbative nationalism, showing aggression towards progressive and open projections of the future.

The utopias of peace and plenitude promised by past religious or secular movements outlining the model community leading a radically different life to an oppressive past and present find little traction today. They seem implausible to a better-informed contemporary public sceptical of the promise of the blueprint community, warned off by passing knowledge of failed historical attempts to create model cities, religious communities and ideological nations. It is hard to imagine public interest in utopian visions such as Edward Bellamy's in the late nineteenth century that inspired many political causes and their publics long into the twentieth century by mapping the plentiful, just and fraternal order of the future (Lizárraga, 2021). Their details of the ideal society would be met with incredulity or indifference, and their promises of undisturbed happiness and prosperity would be considered an impossible dream or possible nightmare. Such mistrust has tarnished the credibility of an aesthetics of political end points and journeying modes, its appeal confined to communities in some way already disposed to the promises of religious or ideological faith. Only a semiotic residue lingers, as Muhammad Zuberi (2019) illustrates in discussing a heated dispute between believers and sceptics in once-socialist Bangladesh about whether a digital image of the moon resembling a prominent cleric's face confirmed his wisdom and authority. At stake was the veracity of the image as indisputable truth, not its place in stimulating public reflection on secular and religious designs on the country's future.

Christian Sorace (2020) offers a similar interpretation of Maoist revival in China through a managed aesthetics of images and sayings of Mao, Party straplines, state-approved works of art, philosophy and literature, and manuals of customary manners. In this aesthetics, there is nothing of the utopia of rupture and freedom, only the incorporation of Maoist symbols and credos into Xi Jinping's regime's ambitions of nationalist revival based in the synthesis of state-managed capitalism and China's communist legacy (Benney, 2020). Through iconic signs of managed intimacy between the state and the people, the Chinese authorities have resurrected a utopian journey of destiny while concealing clearances and amending waymarks along the way in service of the fiction of achieving the perfect social order. Maoist signs have folded seamlessly into China's consolidation as a spectacle society in which mass use apps promote commodity fetishism, aimless surfing, self-centredness and amorous pursuit (Wu, 2020), reciprocally depoliticizing social life by leaving care of the future to the Chinese communist/commodity state. In this utopia of signs, the Chinese future is a promise of continuity entrusted to the all-knowing state.

The utopian aesthetic, in the few places it survives, has become a hollow sign stripped of any message to citizens to break from tradition, reclaim power, mobilize for a fairer future. It bears no pedagogy of radical newness and change interested in the utopian as an open and evolving journey of hope with others out of an unjust present (Jacoby, 2005). Instead, the purpose of its posters, films, novels, songs, speeches, pamphlets, paintings and plays is one of numbing conformity, not moral awakening and political organization in pursuit of radical change. Little survives of the impetus for aesthetic invention to inaugurate the new, in the way of Fodéba Keïta's ballet, music and poetry that subtly mixed traditional African art forms with communist precepts to build popular interest in the cultural politics of the first government under Sékou Touré after Guinea's liberation from France in 1958. During this brief moment of post-independence democracy, Keïta's art projects tried combine popular interest in Guinean traditions suppressed under colonial rule and a pedagogy of socialist modernity breaking the shackles of colonial oppression (Smith, 2017). The utopian ideal was to make old African traditions and new socialist ideas reverberate, echoing Fanon's rallies and essays for an African nationalism to oust colonial rule and an anti-capitalist internationalism to prevent the formation of a divisive national bourgeoise after independence. Recognizing the corrosions of both colonialism and capitalism, it saw no contradiction between a political aesthetics of national Black consciousness and that of international socialist solidarity (Bose, 2019).

Something of this productive discrepancy can be seen in contemporary ideas of 'progressive nationalism' opposed to the xenophobia of nativist nationalism in Europe while reclaiming its hostility to neoliberal globalization and the disenfranchisement of settled majorities. One proposal of interest to the British New Left has been Tom Nairn's defence of a Scottish and English nationalism rooted in a culture of radical class dissent rather than colonial or anti-colonial nostalgia. This is intended as a popular but cosmopolitan nationalism carried by traditions of anti-elitist dissent and cultural pride without aggressive intentions, assured enough to engage internationally with others on equal terms for emancipatory change (Wellings and Kenny, 2019). It proposes a delicate course between a politics of national pride and engaged internationalism, reminiscent of discussion a century ago between the Jewish philosopher Martin Buber and the socialist Gustav Landauer on affinities between a Judaic understanding of home in nation and diaspora, and the promises of an egalitarian international socialism (Mendes-Flohr, 2019). Both thinkers, united in their opposition to national Zionism and scientific Marxism, thought that national liberation movements committing to transcendental religious or political beliefs would avert a populism of closed borders and sequestered culture. Perhaps progressive nationalism stands a better chance of confronting nativism on its own terms, yet its confidence in a culture of popular dissent harnessed to internationalism seems misplaced at this time of acute global crisis and insecurity meeting with largely secessionist responses. Its politics of national pride and the forgotten people risks straying all too close to nativist nationalism.

Compared to the futurity of utopian nationalism, the projections of romantic and civic nationalism or patriotism have been more preservationist in turning to a past of distinctive landscapes or cultural traditions. If nineteenth-century European romantic nationalism leaned towards preindustrial nature and folk culture to propose an old way of life against the encroachments of modernity, the civic nationalism of the twentieth century – toned down today by progressives as patriotic pride to disarm nativism – sought out distinctive cultural values and dispositions to define and bind the plural modern nation. Though the two vary considerably in their myths of nation, degrees of inwardness and identity markers, they both look to inherent national characteristics to define and bind together the nation of many parts, communities and interests. In this sense, they are on the same ground as nativist nationalism, fighting a battle over 'true' national identity, one whose public reception tips, as argued below, in favour of nativism's rebarbative narrative of indigenous betrayal stoking the resentment of majorities feeling displaced in their 'own' land.

The romantic nationalism driving German unification in the nineteenth century is a good example of tradition recovered for nationhood. Liah Greenfeld (2019) argues that the advocates of German romanticism rejected Enlightenment ideas of the rights-based cosmopolitan community for a more popular vision of a dispersed people united and empowered by state sovereignty, myths of shared custom and common cultural traditions straddling differences of class, city, countryside, language, ethnicity and piety. They saw the politically new and the culturally old coming together to give the states unified into a single nation an organic wholeness. There was a similar romance of oneness in the Mazzinian idea of the nation during the struggle for Italian unification around the same time, projecting a strong and prosperous people's state freed from foreign domination, religious superstition and aristocratic rule, and sustained by popular support for the sentiments and institutions of national rebirth and republicanism (Rowley, 2012). Elsewhere, landscape featured more prominently, for example in popular mid-nineteenth-century Scandinavian novels invoking the Gothic landscape, old attachments to the land, dramas of regional borders crossed and wisdoms of rural witchcraft and folklore. In an epic but sober narrative style, the romantic novels allied the Nordic world and situated its nations in the distinctions of a historical landscape and its country ways (Bohlin, 2021). Along with landscape art portraying rugged survival in the magic of misty mountains and the open countryside as uniquely Swedish or Norwegian, the novels invested nationalist designs crafted in urban centres with emotional and visual power reaching across the vast distances and differences of a country. Across Europe, the myths of national unity, with their romance of ancient peoples, landscapes and traditions glossed over inconvenient truths of colonial expansion and internal division, much as it does today, as Julia Bennett (2019) shows in her analysis of promotional campaigns in north-west England selling an Englishness of bucolic landscapes and rural traditions stripped of the region's history of slavery, empire and industrial working-class misery.

Civic nationalism's aesthetic of belonging has tended to be more sedate, fixing on political or ethical principles of freedom and the shared life considered important in a society's modern history. It treads the thin line between nation and nationalism, tilting one way or the other depending on the degree of public anxiety over national wellbeing and security. In a recent evocation, Yael Tamir (2019, 2020) argues that liberal politics, confronted by a fundamentalist or nativist politics that thrives on popular feelings of displacement and exploits crises such as the Covid-19 pandemic to sow further discord and division, ought to work the same territory by invoking a patriotism of the protective state, civic freedom, participatory democracy and egalitarian virtue. It is a call to progressive politics to develop an explicit narrative of national belonging and to generate public interest in a liberal patriotism of operative democracy, rule of law and guaranteed individual and group rights, protected by national acceptance of tolerance, fairness and respect as core societal values. Yet the success of attempts to capture the imagination in this way has been modest, illustrated by the failure of progressive parties to steal electoral ground from nativist parties when proposing liberal political and cultural traditions as the core of being British, Swedish, Italian, American or Indian. The propositions have failed to fire the imagination and passion of the discontented, who seem more persuaded by nativist labelling of liberal values and their protagonists as the cause of their marginalization.

Perhaps this is a failure of inadequate aesthetic and affective imagination. The formative years of the welfare state, born out of war and poverty in Europe, displayed a crafted aesthetics of national renewal and unity carried by persuasive campaigns for public schooling, health care, housing, industry and infrastructure. The campaigns captivated populations betrayed by a legacy of war, privatism and class rule who could easily have turned to more sinister protections after the horrors of fascism. The same can be said for the republican nationalism of newly independent postcolonial states that stirred strong passions for tradition harnessed to secular democracy, racial equality and collective modernization: the kind of nationalism that interested Fanon and liberation movements in Africa and Asia that invested in public projects of all manner while encouraging popular arts of national birth, unity and progress that wrapped the new with hope and desire. Contemporary civic nationalism has little of this vigour of conviction (that admittedly did not take long to sour) when asking for tolerance and fairness during xenophobic escalations, defending the provisioning state during moments of national insecurity and crisis, and citing liberal traditions to win over the left-behind. Compared to early post-war decades, there is no world-making art of the civic nation, no portrait of a diverse population universally protected and united in its differences, only sketches of ruptures when periods of crisis reveal the fractures that need healing (Stråth, 2017). The sketches are gestural performances of freedom, rather like images constantly circulated in South Africa of Nelson Mandela in the absence of comprehensive action to address South Africa's continuing oppressions of race, gender and class (Hook, 2017).

What endures is a commemorative, not programmatic, aesthetics of civic nation, typified by ceremonies such as Norway's Nation Day celebrations that perform national identity as plural and inclusive (Buxrud and Fangen, 2017) but leave the rest of the year to romance with old Nordic romantic imagery of a historic people working a rugged landscape. Elsewhere, national events seek to unite a divided population around a story of national liberation, as do National Day commemorations in Burkina Faso, Côte d'Ivoire and Ghana (N'Guessan et al., 2017), but these acts of unity too are ephemeral, a substitute for tangible effort — backed by an appropriate aesthetics — to deliver the nation of and for its plural people. In France, François Hollande's plea for unity behind the values of French republicanism after the deadly 2015 terrorist attacks in Paris moved the nation in its moment of collective grief, but did little to amend the denial of culture, citizenship and equality to France's Arab and post-colonial population despite its slogan of 'fraternity, equality and liberty' (Bogain, 2019). In America, the playbook of civic nation has been similar, one example being John F. Kennedy's evocation in 1960 of America as youthful, changing and progressive to court younger white generations and Black Americans with civil rights promises held back after his election victory by the realities of looming war and delayed social reforms (Corrigan, 2020). Another example half a century later is Barack Obama's challenge to voters in 2008 to have the 'audacity to hope', a slogan that rallied many Americans against the Bush government's record of foreign invasion, cronyism, austerity and racial and class disharmony, but became tarnished after his election victory by neoliberal and foreign policy continuities as well as Black and working-class disappointments (Corrigan, 2020). In both cases the imagery of unity captured an electoral moment but not a continuity of repair in the civic nation.

This contradiction is mirrored in US sponsorship of American jazz overseas as a form of soft diplomacy. State-funded tours in sensitive geopolitical areas showcased the American way of life as free and inclusive, and encouraged genuine musical exchanges while glossing over racial segregation in America behind the façade of celebrating Black musicians (Raussert, 2018). The Jazz Ambassador tours of the 1950s and 1960s attracted massive audiences eager to see the greats of post-war jazz including famous Black musicians, but their symbolism of American optimism and goodwill concealed neo-imperial ambitions abroad and racism at home. Similarly, the Rhythm Road tours launched by the Bush administration in 2005 to court countries suspicious of the US through collaborative music ventures proved to be genuinely reciprocal, yet barely concealed the hypocrisy of a charm offensive while hostilities towards the Arab world continued after 9/11. Here was a Republican diplomacy with none of the naked aggression of its later Trumpian garb, but it glossed over the heavy footprint of racial biopolitics and expansionary geopolitics in America. The engineering of civility in this way may help to ease difficult tensions of diversity and difference, as might etiquette courses that German municipalities put on to foster an ethic of welcome towards displaced migrants (Prvački, 2020), or 'convivencia' cultural events sponsored in Ceuta to ease tensions between its population of Christians, Muslims and Hindus (Campbell, 2018). But it is civility of the moment, rather like the citizenship course in a school that catches the attention of the keen pupil, but loses its teaching in the melee of the schoolyard and beyond.

These are not reasons to criticize attempts to reinvigorate the lacklustre political aesthetics of civic nation, only to question whether they can match the affective force of nativist exploitation of the rage of a disaffected population told their 'stolen' rights and traditions can be restored by ousting migrants, minorities, elites, cosmopolitans, liberals and the foreign in general. Nativism's targets of the recoverable future are clearly mapped, as is its imagery of the old country meeting the needs and desires of its historic people. Its sentiments of majority betrayal and just dues outweigh the milder stays of civic nationalism. This is why the masses rally behind the vitriol and black charm of Le Pen, Trump, Modi, Bolsonaro, Orbán and Meloni, regardless of their inchoate policies that will perpetuate the misery and alienation of the people who vote for them. In the vituperative and indignant are reconciled false promise and unmet need, edging public opinion in the gap accentuated by globalization between a nationalism of global engagement and one of neo-tribal withdrawal very much towards the latter (Triandafyllidou, 2020). Nativism exudes a tone of disruptive necessity, of courage and defiance in an unstable and calamitous present, its iconography of cataclysmic redemption reworking public expectation, as W.J.T. Mitchell's (2021) notes of the aesthetics of Trumpian rage. If civic nationalism approaches the threats of climate change, capitalist crisis, artificial intelligence and dangerous viruses with restorative diplomacy intended to de-escalate and repair, nativism covets uncertainty and risk with intent to accelerate them in service of the tribal state, assuring those at threat that further disruption is required to usher in the new.

Nativism's is an aesthetics of rupture to reclaim the past, relying on the hard boot on the hurting foot to lash out, instead of visiting the dispensary for a bandage to hobble along. That is the appeal of the rebarbative, trading on honed reflexes of aversion to the designated contaminated body (Amin, 2012; Carney, 2015), typified by the Australian Defence League's aggression in December 2005 on Cronulla Beach in Sydney, when its members attacked 'Lebanese' beachgoers in retaliation for an altercation a week before between some lifeguards and a group of Middle Eastern men. Liam Gillespie (2020) argues that the attack expressed a male narcissism of taking on the nation's defence as willing soldiers against growing migrant encroachment, its audacity covertly applauded by many white Australians. The same martial subjectivity was displayed by the Bajrang Dal militants encountered in chapter 2, their bodies toned to sweep away an 'effete' liberal elite and 'disbelievers' in the way of the Hindu nation. As Sushant Kishore (2019) shows, a choreography of physical rituals, displays of strength and staged performances of Hindutva righteousness and wrath towards its enemies has been core to the political tactics of RSS, the paramilitary parent of Bajrang Dal formed nearly 100 years ago and affiliated to Modi's BJP (see also Kapila, 2021). In Hindutva spectacles combining shock and awe, military discipline, raw crowd power, rousing language, Hindu mythology and traditional song and costume, contradictory emotions channel into a seamless politics of indignation and retribution that appears, for all its familiar historical imagery, the right course of action to millions of India's Hindus.

In numerous democracies in Asia, the Americas and Europe, nativist nationalism, whether state-sponsored or otherwise, has found mass support for a vengeful politics precisely through such forms of aesthetic labour making the harmful seem right, urgent, playful. It has rediscovered an old playbook of news, fiction, film and sound constantly reworked to stoke fear, awe and enthralment. In addition to the cultural industriousness of German Nazism and Italian Fascism, the early forays of the Franco regime into light-hearted films romanticizing the heroic or stoic subject and popular folklore come to mind (Labanyi, 2019) along with its later arts naturalizing traditional gender roles, anti-republicanism, nationalist pride and conservative etiquette (Hernández Burgos, 2021). The choreographing of nationalist righteousness through popular participatory arts eased the passage of the regime's rout of all that it considered degenerate and inimical to Francoism. Then, and today, there was no cultural response of similar strength from anti-nationalist movements. In an interesting twist, Christopher Grobe (2020) argues that the contemporary Alt-Right has stolen the stage tactics of the post-'68 critical Left, in drawing on managed shock, ridicule, humour and caricature to mock and belittle its opponents while presenting its own case with blokey lightness and self-irony. The tactics have made the Left look ponderous and sulky and the Right optimistic and fun-loving, capitalizing on public weariness with daily forecasts of existential collapse. They have enabled a politics of rebarbative nationalism to steal the shine of past utopian and romantic nationalist projects and to make the more familiar politics of civic patriotism seem dull and inadequate. They have understood why it matters to think of the political as the circulation of affects, moods and atmospheres, worked into everyday sentiments of belonging, as Angharad Closs Stephens (2022) shows in her study of contemporary British nationalism.

What aesthetic options remain open for a counter-politics of plural coexistence in this situation? Given the popularity of the nationalist imaginary, it would be tempting to suggest a stronger aesthetics of the civic nation reinforcing public belief in the necessity of the open and interactive society cohering around shared political or ethical principles. Yet, as already suggested, this image is tarnished and of less interest to hard-done majorities attracted to the promise of a golden future brought by the hard-cleansed nation. The aesthetic effort, of course, could be stepped up through an affective pedagogy of civic nation mobilizing public art, song, drama, film and other cultural forms, and around sentiments of self-irony, hope and warmth, to recall Grobe. But this may not be enough to match the tonal shifts achieved by nativist populism. It may pay to open a different aesthetic politics of common existence, one that projects the relational nation that already exists – or has to exist – for the wellbeing of the many. Here, aesthetic attention would focus on public care for the cohabited plural nation requiring worldliness and common endeavour to survive the threat of collective existential collapse, citing extant and imagined diplomacies and collaborations amid division and deprivation – the forms of urban encounter, interactive democracy, publicness, shared space and collective provision illustrated in this book. From the citations of shared coexistence could emerge a map of belonging tracing multiple geographies of affiliation, its visualized local and cosmopolitan connections putting into doubt the imagery of tribal nation, its volume of minor breaches no longer seeming improbable or anomalous but necessary for survival. This could be a possible slow-burn aesthetics of relational contiguity dislodging the identity fixtures of sensory nationalism.

Aesthetics of Breach

In his book *Out of the Dark Night*, Achille Mbembe (2021) places side by side a sweeping chapter on the fragilities of today's planetary condition and one on French republicanism's occlusion of a history of colonial violence, plantation servitude and racial suppression. Scanning the infractions of global capitalism, technological innovation, planetary exhaustion, neo-imperial exploitation and international inequality, the first chapter proposes a decolonial ethos to grasp and repair these dislocations, citing Africa's long negotiation of precarity and subjugation through fugitive solidarities and improvised forms of creativity. The second chapter, looking past the French republican fantasy of community, proposes a political aesthetic of being-in-common respectful of plural singularities, the incommensurable and proximity without enforced reciprocity. Joining these two very different chapters is the proposition that to live in difference – national and international – requires a decolonial politics of repair and affinity with nature, the distant stranger and the violated. For Mbembe, a decolonial optic opens the possibility of equitable and respectful coexistence among humans and with nature, echoing Paul Gilroy's (2016) ideas on reparative humanism referenced earlier in the book.

Similarly, asking how breaches in the rebarbative and racist present could be amplified, Judith Butler (2018) proposes a kinship of 'susceptibility' between subjects disidentifying with 'white time' – subordinated women, Black and other displaced people and youths whose futures have been stolen opening to each other and showing the desirability of new ways of living together. The aesthetics of breach against nationalism outlined in this section is in sympathy with the thinking of Mbembe, Gilroy and Butler on decolonial and minor disidentifications.

The archive of minor aesthetics of belonging is much richer than publicly acknowledged. At the end of the nineteenth century amid continuing violence towards African Americans after the abolition of slavery, a little-remembered movement emerged encouraging freed slaves to move to wholly Black new towns in rural America. The 'Black Towns' were advertised as an opportunity to set up home, property and business in self-managed settlements shielded from the influence and control of White America. As the towns grew, their social structures became more differentiated and gaps appeared between older and wealthier owners yielding power and newer and poorer residents without means or influence. Yet the towns maintained the 'image and ideology' of a united community protecting its own, valuing moral education and decency, and enabling Black uplift (Crockett, 1979). Whatever their contradictions, the towns defied White catachrestic fantasies of blackness as an empty sign to be filled by master overseers, by offering a rich imagery of Black emancipation, identity and self-rule (Warren, 2018). This is one of many instances of affirmative Black fugitivity in the history of America written out of the national narrative (cf. Hartmann, 2019, for an account of the exuberant defiance of young Black women pioneering new lives in American cities in the first decades of the twentieth century). From a very different time and place, but no less significant in its quiet defiance of racist defilement, is the art produced by Esther Kvinitz in the late twentieth century, encapsulating her trauma as a Jewish girl on the run from Nazi occupation in Poland. In thirty-six elaborate needlepoint panels of everyday rural life, the adult Kvinitz wove her fear of persecution into floral scenes of farming and a child's playscapes, eschewing victimhood by giving the panels an elegiac tone of defiance towards Nazi atrocity in her village, including her family (Adelman and Kozol, 2016).

The Black Towns and Kvinitz's art exemplify a long archive of survivor generativity in the face of deforming power. Its public recognition would add weight to similar contemporary initiatives and also shift opinion on the imagined past. In his book *Afro-Fabulations*, Tavia Nyong'o (2018) shows how interactive art installations of times of past Black oppression and resistance in America can enliven this history as a form of commemorative empowerment and reappraisal of the stories of nation. Similarly, Jennifer Nash (2018) digs into the complicity of law in the history of Black deaths in America, to propose an intersectional politics of law and love to unite a fractured contemporary Black politics and open it to other sufferers of institutional violence. Nash suggests that awareness of America's deep record of institutional injustice would nudge Black feminism towards demanding comprehensive legal reforms and making alliances with other marginalized communities, in the process opening mainstream America to a politics of intersectional justice. The challenge posed to progressive causes by this kind of academic inquiry is to invent charismatic ways of connecting and amplifying the archive – historical and contemporary – of submerged projects of care, slowly altering public understanding of the record of community and nation. One example is a new genre of European feminist films capturing 'intimate connection [and] momentary happiness and community' behind 'the structures that stand in the way' (Stehle and Weber, 2020: 152). Describing one film of forced migrants facing continual displacement and state violence, Maria Stehle and Beverly Weber tell us about how 'Fariba/Siamak and Anne make love just before Fariba is deported; Lotte and Ayten touch hands across the empty space of the detention cell; Manu and Abbas dance on the train just before Abbas gets arrested; Myriam and Nour pray together in their respective languages as their voices are drowned out by falling bombs' (2020: 152). The portrait of human connection in situations of extreme precarity and danger – more so across divisions of nationality, sexuality, gender and ethnicity – makes nativist talk of migrant encroachment and contamination seem senseless.

There is a fringe film culture that merits mainstream expansion, allied to other art forms. Consider just the history of subversive and alternative street art. Commenting on Istanbul and Athens, Julia Tulke (2019) sees such art locating public defiance of power in fraught political moments into a dissenting tradition legitimating the right and obligation to oppose. As a mnemonic of peripheral demand from many quarters, it offers no automatic path to the 'right cause', as Jim Aulich (2019) shows in his study of public art since the French Revolution encapsulating many political demands, from the anarchic to the liberal. This is why some street art projects stage their pedagogic intent, one contemporary example being 'The Hill' community arts project in a poor mixed neighbourhood in Copenhagen, which avoided art romanticizing intercultural encounter in preference for temporary installations in public space of local life by artists working with or adjacent to playing children. The project considered the adjacency of art and play to be a better stimulant of local social curiosity and interaction than artistic hand-downs of multicultural community (Illeris, 2015). The interactive forms of pedagogic theatre work in much the same way, be they participatory stage performances of the climate crisis to move audiences into action (e.g. Bruno Latour's play *Global Gaia Circus* witnessing the cries of a distressed earth), or dramas of 'legislative theatre' following Augusto Boal's pioneering work with peasants in rural Peru and Argentina, in which professional actors work with conflicted communities to stage and debate local grievances (Coppola, 2020).

These examples merely hint at a vast body of pedagogic art rejecting the aesthetics of a biopolitics of isolation and aversion through disclosures of the lived as a connective of sutured fragments (McFarlane, 2021). An expanded canvas of affirmative relations would begin to reorient public feelings of abandonment and betrayal towards the interactive and common. Take, for example, the potentiality of citizen testimonies locked in the digital archive of civic mobilization based on social collaboration against state and militia violence, as Katarzyna Ruchel-Stockmans (2021) has shown for the Arab Spring uprisings and the Syrian conflict. Sensitive public airing of such testimony – from the Syrian Archive, Forensic Architecture's reconstructions of Israeli state violence and other archives of critical scrutiny – would facilitate the circulation of counter-currents of civic collaboration beyond the fringe and reinforce a public susceptibility of fellowship and collective justice. One illustration is the work of anti-racist movements in Peru and Argentina encouraging the poor to photograph their lives, thus folding the causes of racial and class justice together and into popular momentum against a long history of maldistributed power and opportunity (Oliart and Triquell, 2019). If the challenge of the critical arts is to encapsulate scattered evidence of social opposition to isolation and aversion, that of progressive politics is to want to know and be clear about how to mobilize it to alter popular culture.

It is a challenge of intercepting established conventions and institutions operating as the hidden apparatus of manufactured consensus, one that offers slack to the hegemonic but requires the subaltern to find an infrastructure able to make its nascency ordinary. To cite George Perec's book *The Infraordinary*, some literary styles possess this 'endotic' ability to make the imperceptible details of everyday space and social gesture seem culturally salient. Daryl Martin (2019) identifies this ability in Perec's own novels and in the work of Jonathan Meades, respectively defining Frenchness and Englishness from meanings made in ordinary settings and atmospheres, in people's everyday curiosities of place and social interaction. The endotic is a cultivated art form able to quietly alter received wisdom by making the peripheral seem sensible and significant. It does more than translate and legitimate, in contrast to the work of countless professional and lay creatives today working sophisticated digital art packages to popularize nativist resentment or liberal conviviality. A clear example is the cartographic art of the celebrated French geographer Paul Vidal de la Blache. Dana Lindaman (2017) argues that when de la Blache delved into new cinema techniques in the early twentieth century to change cartographic convention by introducing images of regional ways of life, he radically altered public perception of the geography of the nation and national belonging. His new Atlas replaced the republican portrait of a unitary France, divided into neat administrative units with their own settlements and distances from Paris, with an organic encapsulation of the country's spatial form and identity. Without maps of the physical terrain divorced from human and natural characteristics, the Atlas visualized a France of lived milieus with distinctive identities shaped by local connections of nature and culture but also part of a nation of shared traditions, landscapes and infrastructures exceeding the integrations of administration and politics. As the educational and popular influence of the Atlas grew, the French came to identify with a different France; a republic of distinctive regional identities. The cartographic invention had transformed France's understanding of itself.

There are other examples of endotic art. They include the iterations of library cataloguing across alphabetical, numerical and thematic classification systems, which united collections separated by time, space and culture, in the process creating affinity or distance between works on the basis of their place in the index (Rieder, 2020). Library cataloguing became culturally consequential through what it listed, made available and juxtaposed, raising pertinent questions about its role prior to the digital age (which has opened multiple and flexible ways of gathering and sorting texts) in shaping the relative influence of conformist and dissident knowledge in different reading cultures. The history of measurement provides another example. Modern economies have become performance societies guided by indicators of progress and preparedness in all areas of social life, worked deep into computational models and algorithms to forecast futures and map scenarios from vast quantities of data. Christina Boswell (2018) argues that indicators have become the measure of efficacy, value and worth, and the window onto the future, framing public and policy and expectation of what counts and where things are heading. They drive decisions and plans, their mastery confers power and influence, they serve vying interests and causes, and their results are keenly anticipated and vigorously debated by stakeholders. They have become an indispensable infrastructure of government and opposition, prompting Boswell to wonder if public suspicion of elites and experts drummed up by nativists for malign purposes could be channelled in different political directions under a more democratic measurement culture routinely disclosing methodological assumptions and incorporating measures of social value and preference into its metrics.

An aesthetics of breach developing endotic art forms to figure the minor, convivial and relational could also, finally, find ways of convincing publics of the necessity of cooperation between strangers at home and abroad to protect the severely threatened commons. The imagery of urgency is already there, graphically illustrated by satellite pictures of a distressed Earth and by other visual media showing the drama of melting ice caps, destroyed habitats and species, extreme weather events and mass misery and migration linked to the climate crisis and capitalist profligacy. The dangers of a disappearing planetary commons are widely known as is the outline of what needs to be done to safeguard the future. Beyond a small but powerful coterie of vested interests and naysayers, publics and policymakers around the world know that in facing end times, societies must switch to live ethically and sustainably, adopt green technologies and renewable energy, and reduce dependency on fossil fuels. There is a clear imagery of survival based on rewilding, vegetarianism, sustainable farming, green urbanism, consumer and producer parsimony, renewable energy, decarbonization and deglobalization. Its mobilization remains dangerously constrained by corporate and political inertia and by the powers and habits of carbon and petrochemical capitalism (Malm, 2018; Hanieh, 2021), yet its percolations into the collective unconscious are indisputable. In these percolations, an aesthetics of environmental preparedness through inclusive and joint address of risk and vulnerability might help to strengthen public resolve to ensure change, its ethos of common care and global responsibility unmasking the hapless narcissism of a nativist politics of secession and self-interest (Hage, 2017).

The task here is to add form, colour and vitality to the metaphysics of interdependence articulated by Alfred North Whitehead, William James and, latterly, Bruno Latour (Weber, 2016). It is to make common through imaginative and accessible art forms, public feel for the lifeforce of interacting bodies and cultures, air and soil, atoms and molecules, heat and cold, water and energy, infrastructures and institutions, metabolic circuits and living matter, maintaining one and all here and elsewhere. It is to curate a powerful sense of common stewardship of this lifeforce through respectful and convivial coexistence, and of the dire consequences of connections broken in the extinction of nonhuman life and in the exclusion of proximate and distant humans. The art forms exist in liminal form, such as experiments in immersive art offering sensory experience of interdependencies of biology and nature sustaining human life and culture. In her study of such experiments in Latin America engaging with the insights of science, Joanna Page (2021) describes artworks engendering care for the air by expressing the distress of a polluted atmosphere, visualizing synthetic biology experiments showing how slowly and painfully damaged nature repairs itself, performing the geological record to decentre anthropomorphic time and obsession, and showing ants and spiders at work to show what cooperation could achieve for humans. Such environmental art foregrounds the extensive connections across time and space enabling human wellbeing and fulfilment, rather like Julie Mehretu's paintings of the global meanders of identity and belonging.

At present this art circulates in restricted circles, but could be expanded much further, also to capture the interactions of lived space traced in this book – the relations of cohabitation and commensality making urban identity (Amin and Lancione, 2022; Barua, 2023), the myriad geographies of affiliation crossing boundaries of tribe and nation, and the lively online and offline sociabilities pushing back at the malign and aggressive. The challenge is to find a constancy of charismatic art forms capturing the public imagination and altering perception of how things are, from the plenitude of relations. When early balloonists risked their lives to float above a crowd of nervous strangers, the further they rose up, the more the crowd appeared as a single body in its landscape willing their survival (Pearl, 2019). Today the possibilities of aerial capture of the details of assemblage on the Earth's surface that defy the givens of nation and community are immense. Similarly, the images of genomic science diving into the composites of life reveal genes-in-relation complicity nudging the commonalities and differences of individual and collective subjectivity (Bassett et al., 2020). From scans of the inner human enabled by new imaging technologies in psychology and biology is emerging a story worth telling of the folds of culture and ontology that contradict the idea of the pure and autonomous subject (McGilchrist, 2009).

Conclusion

Recognizing the political power of the aesthetics of imagined community, this chapter has focused on arts that could strengthen public affinity with the relational contiguities identified in the book. It has been sceptical of the aesthetics of 'soft' nationalism – liberal, romantic and civic – considering it unable to match the visceral appeal of nativist imagery to majorities seeing themselves sacrificed in their 'own' land, as well as to shake off accusations of its own complicity in the divisions feeding nativism (e.g. the elitism of liberal nation or the bourgeois leanings of civic nation). The argument has turned, instead, to an aesthetics of contiguity naturalizing the plural, interactive and common nation, one that seems barely visible in contemporary progressive politics. The fragile returns of social democracy in nations challenged by nativism seem so by default, relying on scraping numbers from past loyalty, public disappointment with the corruption and incompetence of populist governments, and copycat jingoistic and anti-migration policies. Compared to the force of nativist imagery of threatening elites, minorities and migrants, progressive effort to foster public care for the community of difference, encounter and commonality has been lacklustre. It is as though the energy and courage to imagine nation differently have been crushed by the epoch-making postures of nationalism.

Yet without a passionate aesthetics of the plural nation, nativism's disturbing narrative of national cleansing in the name of majority sovereignty, wellbeing and unity will dig in deeper, its violence normalized. But with no clear model of belonging at hand, as this chapter has suggested, the impetus has to come from finding solidity and shape for practices of coexistence within and between the tested democracies. A new public imagery of belonging could take shape around arts visualizing ordinary encounters, collaborations among communities granted only a 'remaindered life' by power (Tadiar, 2022), the infrastructural, natural and social commons of collective survival, the chains of connection across societies and ecologies whose severance weakens life everywhere, and the archive of words and stories of relational interdependence. From a cultivated aesthetics of minor existence, encounter and commonality could arise that urgency of slow burn, rather like the turn in environmental arts integrating the pessimism of impending doom and the optimism of positive climate mitigations (cf. Vince, 2022). The times demand this, and offer the progressive mainstream a chance to place a new politics of belonging at the heart of its cause. As Judith Butler (2022: 44) writes, reflecting on intensifying planetary inhabitability,

> because certain conditions of life and living are laid bare by the circulation of the virus, we now have a chance to grasp our relations to the earth and to each other in sustaining ways, to understand ourselves less as separate entities driven by self-interest than as complexly bound together in a living world that requires our collective resolve to struggle against its destruction, the destruction of what bears incalculable value – the ultimate sense of the tragic.

Coda

While drafting these last pages, nativist parties emerged victorious in elections in Italy, Sweden and Israel, Putin's justification of the invasion of Ukraine as fraternal liberation continued to find public support in Russia, and the Left returned to power in Brazil by the slimmest of margins despite the chaos created by the ousted nationalist government. And there are few signs of nativism losing mass support in other democracies such as the US, Poland, Hungary, the UK, Turkey and India, run down by divisive nationalist governments. It seems that the more social misery and resentment intensify – exponentially soon from the devastations of climate change and a looming global recession and inflationary crisis exhausting the public purse – the greater grows popular support for rebarbative nationalism. Through worsening times majorities are staying with the fiction of the native nation promising plenitude and pride despite its lies and failure to improve the security and wellbeing of the disaffected. This is because of its affective force as a story of national belonging and becoming, strengthened by the absence of a similarly persuasive counter-narrative. Stunned by nativism's visceral assault on all things liberal, cosmopolitan, rational and deliberative, the progressive mainstream has lost a vanguard ability to give shape to a future that others might desire through appropriate mobilizations of imagined community. In this absence, the victims of market fundamentalism, unequal political economy, oligarchic and oligopolistic profiteering and environmental extraction have gravitated to nativism's drawbridge politics of resentment. Dissent against this politics – in the encounters of everyday life, in campaigns for class, racial and gender justice, environmental sustainability and cultural recognition, and in public opposition to diffuse violence and hate – has struggled to find traction. It has not found a narrative of plural nation with sufficient appeal and institutional weight behind it.

One hundred years ago, reflecting in prison on why an Italy upended by war rejected communist liberation for Fascist populism, Gramsci (1992) proposed a cultural 'war of position' against domination that would reinforce, as Robert Cox (1983: 165) summarizes, 'the social foundations of a new state' by 'creating alternative institutions and alternative intellectual resources within existing society'. In a similar vein, Perry Anderson (2020) suggests that an elite post-war portrait of the European Community as a federation of peace and prosperity played a pivotal role in legitimating its establishment and ensuring its survival through difficult moments of national suspicion in the second half of the twentieth century. These are illustrations of the power in moments of rupture and transition of articulations of imagined community that can carry a different kind of public demand. This is why this book has settled on the cultural politics of belonging, rather than the political economy of general wellbeing, by staging relational contiguity, convivial cohabitation, the public interest and commonality as measures of national unity and worth. It has offered these suggestions as first moves in a new war of position, well aware of the need for influential voices and institutions, imaginative slogans, novel technologies of mobilization, clear diagrams of the good society and strong reciprocities between progressive parties and publics to match the affective force of nativist imaginary. The sites of augmentation are not obvious in the ailing democracies with a weakened progressive mainstream, but the grammar of the common, convivial and intimate across difference, along with civic, legal and institutional resistance to nativist obfuscation and violence, is evident enough in everyday life and organized opposition for the protagonists of progressive politics to make cause.

Much as the book has skirted past political economy, there is little doubt that its ideas on belonging would benefit from reductions in poverty and inequality in the troubled democracies. Nativism thrives on the resentments of deprivation and alienation linking material circumstances and cultural dispositions. It has been said often enough that the political economy of unfettered markets, fiscal and welfare biases towards the well-off and oligarchic profiteering have fanned secessionist, xenophobic and anti-elitist sentiment among majorities let down by resulting deficits of housing, educational, work, income, insurance and welfare security. Across the countries cited in the book, these failings have been felt as a form of abandonment by a system geared towards the privileged and borderless, a perception that could be steered past nativist blaming of equally vulnerable subjects such as migrants and minorities by a political economy of universal security and wellbeing. This would temper the politics of resentment, if new policies were publicly understood to stem from a commitment to growth through social and spatial empowerment, sustainable development and equitable redistribution of wealth. It would make a difference if progressive parties explicitly disowned the economics of trickle-down, welfare parsimony, fiscal minimalism, wealth inequality, free-market rule and profits at any price, that is, their acquiescence over several decades to a growth model based on market sovereignty, concentrated and centralized wealth and state welfare parsimony. Decades of neoliberal governance in and out of austerity have achieved the opposite of generalized wellbeing and security, leaving both the mainstream Right and Left tarnished as complicit in the misery, inequality and alienation exploited by nativists to divide the ethnically and religiously coded left-behind against each other.

Something could be recovered of the forgotten 'social model' of economic management premised on welfare equity, regardless of the intense market pressures and constraints on state autonomy posed by globalization. This includes designs for just-in-case planning and active management and redistribution of growth through public ownership and control, regional and industrial policy, anti-trust laws and income controls. It includes provisions for the most vulnerable and exposed through comprehensive welfare protections, opportunities to enhance skills, capabilities and career opportunities, and participation in workplace schemes, the circular economy and social enterprise. It includes committing to a politics of the whole nation through policies that ensure social and regional cohesion, protect the social contract though graduated taxation and collective bargaining, and incentivize nationwide infrastructural, institutional and service parity. This is not a matter of recovering a blueprint of the social model, not least because of adjustments needed to tackle the threats posed by the environmental emergency, unregulated artificial intelligence, the precarities of the gig economy, new forms of oligarchy corrupting democracy and endlessly escalating existential crises. Yet the premise of a provisioning political economy – updated, extended and considerably democratized as a kind of New Green Deal – can be retained in tackling the grotesque inequalities and social abandonments exacerbated by mixes of neoliberal and corporatist economic management over the last thirty to forty years in the old and new democracies. The delivery across the social and regional spectrum of decent and stable work, welfare and income protections, housing, education and healthcare security, and enabling infrastructures and services, harnessed to a narrative of nation as the ground of convivial cohabitation and open encounter, should help to neutralize the discontent of hard-done majorities. It might even dampen their interest in nativist obsession with borders, minorities and migrants.

Of necessity, the details of the social model will vary between the troubled democracies, depending on their legacies of government and public expectation, the limits of fiscal and financial expansion, the scale and nature of disaffection and social need and the machineries of public delivery. They will also vary by progressive interpretations of the meaning and mechanisms of the protected society, some rooted in directive government and others in civic partnerships, some focusing on the minima of social survival and others on the maxima of social enablement. Considering just the inherited mixes of market, populist and oligarchic rule, the options for progressive parties in Turkey, India or Brazil will not be the same as those in Poland or Hungary or those in the US, Italy and the UK. But the principle of the welfare-led managed economy as the bedrock of social democracy remains valid across the contexts, exemplified by near-universal public endorsement during the pandemic for the caring and protective state, for front-line workers and social solidarity, for social groups and locations at greater risk from the disease, and for professional expertise and evidence-based authority. In turn, the EU's decision to establish the hard-won €1.8 trillion fund to help the hardest affected member states to recover from the pandemic, after more than a decade of offering only biting conditional loans to countries in debt after the 2008 financial crisis, may be a sign of growing policy interest in the social model. But any departure from laissez-faire and welfare parsimony forced by the threat of mass destruction is fragile, easily reversible once market power regroups and crisis recedes, as happened to government declarations in favour of responsible financial management in the early months of the global recession following the 2008 crisis. Swift was the return of unregulated casino finance that precipitated the crisis – a surest reminder that Covid promises of building back better could prove hollow once the normal business returns of global rapaciousness, miserly state protection and copious economic suffering from the pandemic's fallout and global slowdown, once again playing straight into the hands of rebarbative nationalism. The window to invent a new political economy that displaces the exclusionary social state that nativism wants is small indeed.

References

Adelman, R.A. & Kozol, W. (2016). Ornamenting the unthinkable: Visualizing survival under occupation. *Women's Studies Quarterly*, 44(1/2), 171–87.

Airas, I. (2021). Populism as resonance machine: Affect, the Sweden Democrats, and the 2018 Swedish General Election. Unpublished PhD thesis, University of Cambridge.

Airas, I. & Truedsson, C. (2023). Contesting and envisioning 'trygghet': The Sweden Democrats, Social Democrats, and the 2018 Swedish General Election. *Area*, 55(1), 26–37. https://doi.org/10.1111/area.12689

Akbaba, S. (2018). Re-narrating Europe in the face of populism. *Insight Turkey*, 20(3), 199–218.

ALLEA (2018). Loss of trust? Loss of trustworthiness? Truth and expertise today. Discussion Paper. All European Academies.

Amin, A. (2012). *Land of Strangers*. Polity Press.

Amin, A. & Howell, P. (2016). Thinking the commons. In *Releasing the Commons* (pp. 1–17). Routledge.

Amin, A. & Lancione, M. (Eds.) (2022). *Grammars of the Urban Ground*. Duke University Press.

Amin, A. & Richaud, L. (2020). Stress and the ecology of urban experience: Migrant mental lives in central Shanghai.

Transactions of the Institute of British Geographers, 45(4), 862–76.

Amoore, L. (2019). Doubt and the algorithm: On the partial accounts of machine learning. *Theory, Culture & Society*, 36(6), 147–69. https://doi.org/10.1177/0263276419851846

Amoore, L. (2020). *Cloud Ethics: Algorithms and the Attributes of Ourselves and Others*. Duke University Press.

Anderson, P. (2020). The European coup. *London Review of Books*, 42(24), 9–23.

Andrews, L. (2017). How can we demonstrate the public value of evidence-based policy making when government ministers declare that the people 'have had enough of experts'? *Palgrave Communications*, 3(1), 11. https://doi.org/10.1057/s41599-017-0013-4

Ansell, A. (2017). Democracy is a blessing: Phatic ritual and the public sphere in northeast Brazil. *Journal of Linguistic Anthropology*, 27(1), 22–39. https://doi.org/10.1111/jola.12148

Appadurai, A. (2019). Democracy fatigue. In H. Geiselberger (Ed.), *The Great Regression* (pp. 1–12). Polity Press.

Appiah, K.A. (2018). *The Lies That Bind: Rethinking Identity*. Profile Books.

Arendt, H. (2009 [1963]). *On Revolution*. Penguin Books.

Aulich, J. (2019). Conclusion. In A. McGarry, I. Erhart, H. Eslen-Ziya, O. Jenzen & U. Korkut (Eds.), *The Aesthetics of Global Protest* (pp. 269–92). Amsterdam University Press.

Back, L. (2021). Hope's work. *Antipode*, 53(1), 3–20.

Back, L. & Sinha, S. (2018). *Migrant City*. Routledge.

Balibar, É. (2015). *Citizenship*. Polity Press.

Barua, M. (2023). *Living Cities: Reconfiguring Urban Ecologies*. Minnesota University Press.

Bassett, C., Kember, S. & O'Riordan, K. (2020). *Furious*. Pluto Press.

Beaman, J. (2017). *Citizen Outsider: Children of North African Immigrants in France*. University of California Press.

Bennett, J. (2019). Imagining Englishness through contested English landscapes. *European Journal of Cultural Studies*, 22(5–6), 835–48. https://doi.org/10.1177/1367549418786414

Benney, J. (2020). Aesthetic resources in contemporary Chinese politics. *Critical Inquiry*, 46(3), 605–26.

Berlant, L. (2022) *On the Inconvenience of Other People*, Duke University Press.

Bertsou, E. & Caramani, D. (2022). People haven't had enough of experts: Technocratic attitudes among citizens in nine European democracies. *American Journal of Political Science*, 66(1), 5–23. https://doi.org/10.111ajps.12554

Beuret, N. (2017). Review: Isabelle Stengers, *In Catastrophic Times: Resisting the Coming Barbarism*. *Theory, Culture & Society*, 34(7–8), 259–64. https://doi.org/10.1177/0263276417736368

Bhargava, R. (2023). *Between Hope and Despair: 100 Ethical Reflections on Contemporary India*. Bloomsbury.

Biehl, J. (2013). *Vita: Life in a Zone of Social Abandonment*. University of California Press.

Biehl, J. & Locke, P. (2010). Deleuze and the anthropology of becoming. *Current Anthropology*, 51(3), 317–51. https://doi.org/10.1086/651466

Biehl, J.G., Good, B. & Kleinman, A. (Eds.) (2007). *Subjectivity: Ethnographic Investigations*. University of California Press.

Bimber, B. & Gil de Zúñiga, H. (2020). The unedited public sphere. *New Media & Society*, 22(4), 700–15. https://doi.org/10.1177/1461444819893980

Blokland, T. & Nast, J. (2014). From public familiarity to comfort zone: The relevance of absent ties for belonging in Berlin's mixed neighbourhoods. *International Journal of Urban and Regional Research*, 38(4), 1142–59.

Bogain, A. (2019). Terrorism and the discursive construction of national identity in France. *National Identities*, 21(3), 241–65. https://doi.org/10.1080/14608944.2018.1431877

Bohlin, A. (2021). The novel reconsidered: Emotions and anti-realism in mid-19th-century Scandinavian literature. *Nations and Nationalism*, 27(3), 831–45. https://doi.org/10.1111/nana.12698

Bose, A. (2019). Frantz Fanon and the politicization of the Third World as a collective subject. *Interventions*, 21(5), 671–89. https://doi.org/10.1080/1369801X.2019.1585925

Boswell, C. (2018). *Manufacturing Political Trust: Targets and Performance Indicators in Public Policy*. Cambridge University Press.

Bosworth, K. (2019). The people know best: Situating the counterexpertise of populist pipeline opposition movements. *Annals of the American Association of Geographers*, 109(2), 581–92. https://doi.org/10.1080/24694452.2018.1494538

Boyce, T. & Chunnu, W. (2020). *Historicizing Fear*. University Press of Colorado.

Brandmayr, F. (2021). When boundary organisations fail: Identifying scientists and civil servants in L'Aquila earthquake trial. *Science as Culture*, 30(2), 237–60. https://doi.org/10.1080/09505431.2020.1802709

Brincker, B. & Leoussi, A.S. (2018). Anthony D. Smith and the role of art, architecture and music in the growth of modern nations: A comparative study of national parliaments and classical music in Britain and Denmark. *Nations and Nationalism*, 24(2), 312–26. https://doi.org/10.1111/nana.12409

Brown, B. (2020). Re-assemblage (theory, practice, mode). *Critical Inquiry*, 46(2), 259–303.

Bryant, R. & Knight, D.M. (2019). *The Anthropology of the Future*. Cambridge University Press.

Buettner, E. (2016). *Europe after Empire: Decolonization, Society, and Culture*. Cambridge University Press.

Butler, J. (2018). Solidarity/susceptibility. *Social Text*, 36(4), 1–20. https://doi.org/10.1215/01642472-7145633

Butler, J. (2022). *What World Is This?: A Pandemic Phenomenology*. Columbia University Press.

Buxrud, B. & Fangen, K. (2017). Norwegian National Day oratory: Constructing and reconstructing a national we. *Nations and Nationalism*, 23(4), 770–89. https://doi.org/10.1111/nana.12346

Caldeira, T. (2012). Imprinting and moving around: New visibilities and configurations of public space in São Paulo. *Public Culture*, 24(2), 385–419.

Campbell, B. (2018). Having faith in Ceuta: Error and ethics in rituals of/for 'convivencia' in a Spanish enclave in northern Africa. *Journal of Ritual Studies*, 32(2), 27–41.

Camporesi, S., Vaccarella, M. & Davis, M. (2017). Investigating public trust in expert knowledge: Narrative, ethics, and engagement. *Journal of Bioethical Inquiry*, 14(1), 23–30. https://doi.org/10.1007/s11673-016-9767-4

Caraccioli, M.J. (2021). *Writing the New World: The Politics of Natural History in the Early Spanish Empire*. University of Florida Press.

Carney, P. (2015). Foucault's punitive society: Visual tactics of marking as a history of the present. *The British Journal of Criminology*, 55(2), 231–47.

Carter, P. (2013). *Meeting Place: The Human Encounter and the Challenge of Coexistence*. University of Minnesota Press.

Castells, M. (2015). *Networks of Outrage and Hope: Social Movements in the Internet Age*, 2nd edn. Polity.

Chakrabarty, D. (2019). The planet: An emergent humanist category. *Critical Inquiry*, 46(1), 1–31.

Chatterjee, M. (2016). *Bandh* politics: Crowds, spectacular violence, and sovereignty in India. *Distinktion: Journal of Social Theory*, 17(3), 294–307. https://doi.org/10.1080/1600910X.2016.1258586

Chatterjee, M. (2023). *The Composition of Violence: The Limits of Exposure and the Making of Minorities*. Duke University Press.

Chatterjee, P. (2011). *Lineages of Political Society: Studies in Postcolonial Democracy*. Columbia University Press.

Chatterjee, P. (2019). *I Am the People: Reflections on Popular Sovereignty Today*. Columbia University Press.

Chin, R. (2017). *The Crisis of Multiculturalism in Europe*. Princeton University Press.

Chlup, R. (2021). National myths and rebounding violence. *Nations and Nationalism*, 27(4), 943–59. https://doi.org/10.1111/nana.12720

Claviez, T. (2016). A metonymic community? Toward a poetics of contingency. In T. Claviez (Ed.), *The Common Growl: Toward a Poetics of Precarious Community* (pp. 39–56). Fordham University Press.

Closs Stephens, A. (2022). *National Affects: The Everyday Atmospheres of Being Political*. Bloomsbury.

Cohn, J.S. (2020). The fantastic from counterpublic to public imaginary: The darkest timeline? *Science Fiction Studies*, 47(3), 448–63. https://doi.org/10.5621/sciefictstud.47.3.0448

Conley, V.A. (2016). The care of the possible. *Cultural Politics*, 12(3), 339–54. https://doi.org/10.1215/17432197-3648894

Connolly, W.E. (2017). *Aspirational Fascism: The Struggle for Multifaceted Democracy under Trumpism*. University of Minnesota Press.

Connolly, W.E. (2019). *Climate Machines, Fascist Drives, and Truth*. Duke University Press.

Coppola, A. (2020). Latour and balloons: Gaïa global circus and the theater of climate change. *Configurations*, 28(1), 29–49. https://doi.org/10.1353/con.2020.0001

Corrigan, L.M. (2020). *Black Feelings: Race and Affect in the Long Sixties*. University Press of Mississippi.

Cox, R.W. (1983). Gramsci, hegemony and international relations: An essay in method. *Millennium*, 12(2), 162–75.

Crichton, M. (2005). *State of Fear*. HarperCollins.

Crockett, N.L. (1979). *The Black Towns*. Regents Press of Kansas.

Cruz-Santiago, A. (2020). Lists, maps, and bones: The untold journeys of citizen-led forensics in Mexico. *Victims & Offenders*, 15(3), 350–69. https://doi.org/10.1080/15564886.2020.1718046

Darling, J. & Wilson, H.F. (2016). *Encountering the City: Urban Encounters from Accra to New York*. Routledge.

Das, V. (2015). *Affliction*. Fordham University Press.

Das, V. (2017). Companionable thinking. *Medicine Anthropology Theory*, 4(3), 191–203. https://doi.org/10.17157/mat.4.3.486

Das, V. (2022). *Slum Acts*. Polity Press.

Dasgupta, S. (2019). *Awakening Bharat Mata: The Political Beliefs of the Indian Right*. Penguin

Davies, W. (2021). Anti-equivalence: Pragmatics of post-liberal dispute. *European Journal of Social Theory*, 24(1), 44–64. https://doi.org/10.1177/1368431020945841

Davis, A. (2019). *Political Communication: A New Introduction for Crisis Times*. Polity.

Davis, M. (2021). The online anti-public sphere. *European Journal of Cultural Studies*, 24(1), 143–59. https://doi.org/10.1177/1367549420902799

De Boeck, F. & Baloji, S. (2016). *Suturing the City. Living Together in Congo's Urban Worlds*. Autograph ABP.

De Genova, N. (2018). The 'migrant crisis' as racial crisis: Do black lives matter in Europe? *Ethnic and Racial Studies*, 41(10), 1765–82.

de Jong, J. & Andeweg, B. (2011). Professionalizing speech production. Changes in 15 years of ministerial speeches. In T. van Haaften, H. Jansen, J. de Jong & W. Koetsenruijter (Eds.), *Bending Opinion: Essays on Persuasion in the Public Domain* (pp. 159–83). Leiden University Press.

de Souza, P. (2020). Sonic archives of breathlessness. *International Journal of Communication*, 14, 5686–704.

Dean, M. (2017). Political acclamation, social media and the public mood. *European Journal of Social Theory*, 20(3), 417–34. https://doi.org/10.1177/1368431016645589

Dellmann, S. (2018). *Images of Dutchness: Popular Visual Culture, Early Cinema and the Emergence of a National Cliché*. Amsterdam University Press.

Delmotte, F., Mercenier, H. & Van Ingelgom, V. (2017). Belonging and indifference to Europe: A study of young people in Brussels. *Historical Social Research/Historische Sozialforschung*, 42(4), 227–49.

Demossier, M. (2017). From the European puzzle to a puzzled Europe. In A. Lerman (Ed.), *Do I Belong?* (pp. 54–69). Pluto Press.

Dewey, J. (2012 [1927]). *The Public and Its Problems: An Essay in Political Inquiry*. Pennsylvania State University Press.

Dolan, F.M. (2018). *Allegories of America*. Cornell University Press.

Dommett, K. & Pearce, W. (2019). What do we know about public attitudes towards experts? Reviewing survey data in the United Kingdom and European Union. *Public Understanding of Science*, 28(6), 669–78. https://doi.org/10.1177/0963662519852038

Duchesne, S. (2018). Who's afraid of banal nationalism? *Nations and Nationalism*, 24(4), 841–56. https://doi.org/10.1111/nana.12457

Duyvendak, J.W. & Kešić, J. (2022). *The Return of the Native: Can Liberalism Safeguard us against Nativism?* Oxford University Press.

Duyvendak, J. & Wekker, F. (2016). At home in the city? The difference between friendship and amicability. In V. Mamadouh & A. van Wageningen (Eds.), *Urban Europe* (pp. 23–29). Cambridge University Press.

Ekström, A. (2021). Thinking publics, building society: Defining a European era. Unpublished paper, Department of History of Science and Ideas, Uppsala University.

Elias, N. (2010). *The Society of Individuals, Collected Works, Vol. 10*. UCD Press.

Elkin-Koren, N. (2020). Contesting algorithms: Restoring the public interest in content filtering by artificial intelligence. *Big Data & Society*, 7(2), 205395172093229. https://doi.org/10.1177/2053951720932296

Elsheikh, D. & Lilleker, D.G. (2021). Egypt's feminist counterpublic: The re-invigoration of the post-revolution public sphere. *New Media & Society*, 23(1), 22–38. https://doi.org/10.1177/1461444819890576

Esguerra, A. (2019). Future objects: Tracing the socio-material politics of anticipation. *Sustainability Science*, 14(4), 963–71. https://doi.org/10.1007/s11625-019-00670-3

Esposito, R. (2019). Postdemocracy and biopolitics. *European Journal of Social Theory*, 22(3), 317–24. https://doi.org/10.1177/1368431019850234

Esposito, R. (2022). *Communitas*. Stanford University Press.

Farrell, H. & Han, H. (2020). Public governance and global politics after COVID-19. In H. Brands & F.J. Gavin (Eds.), *COVID-19 and World Order* (pp. 238–58). Johns Hopkins University Press.

Fast, D. & Moyer, E. (2018). Becoming and coming undone on the streets of Dar es Salaam. *Africa Today*, 64(3), 3–26.

Fenton, N. (2018). Fake democracy: The limits of public sphere theory. *Javnost – The Public*, 25(1–2), 28–34. https://doi.org/10.1080/13183222.2018.1418821

Figueiras, R. (2019). Punditry as a reward system: Audience construction and the logics of the punditry sphere. *Critical Studies in Media Communication*, 36(2), 171–83. https://doi.org/10.1080/15295036.2018.1554256

Fitzgerald, D., Rose, N. & Singh, I. (2016). Revitalizing sociology: Urban life and mental illness between history and the present. *The British Journal of Sociology*, 67(1), 138–60.

Fukuyama, F. (2018). Why national identity matters. *Journal of Democracy*, 29(4), 5–15.

Fuller, M. & Goriunova, O. (2019). *Bleak Joys: Aesthetics of Ecology and Impossibility*. University of Minnesota Press.

Furman, I. & Tunç, A. (2020). The end of the Habermassian ideal? Political communication on Twitter during the 2017 Turkish constitutional referendum. *Policy & Internet*, 12(3), 311–31. https://doi.org/10.1002/poi3.218

García, H. (2019). Reluctant liars? Public debates on propaganda and democracy in twentieth-century Britain (ca. 1914–1950). *Contemporary British History*, 33(3), 383–404. https://doi.org/10.1080/13619462.2019.1571920

Gekker, A. (2019). Playing with power: Casual politicking as a new frame for political analysis. In J. Raessens, S. Lammes, I. Vries & M. de Lange (Eds.), *The Playful Citizen: Civic Engagement in a Mediatized Culture* (pp. 388–419). Amsterdam University Press.

Gest, J. (2015). Reluctant pluralists: European Muslims and essentialist identities. *Ethnic and Racial Studies*, 38(11), 1868–85.

Gillespie, L. (2020). The imagined immunities of defense nationalism. *Political Psychology*, 41(5), 997–1011. https://doi.org/10.1111/pops.12661

Gilroy, P. (2016). Antiracism and (re)humanization. In T. Claviez (Ed.), *The Common Growl: Toward a Poetics of Precarious Community* (pp. 111–36). Fordham University Press.

Glissant, É. (1997). *Poetics of Relation*. University of Michigan Press.

Goffman, E. (2007 [1959]). *The Presentation of Self in Everyday Life*. Penguin Books.

Goodhart, D. (2017). *The Road to Somewhere: The Populist Revolt and the Future of Politics*. Oxford University Press.

Goswami, M. (2020). Benedict Anderson, *Imagined Communities* (1983). *Public Culture*, 32(2), 441–8. https://doi.org/10.1215/08992363-8090180

Gramsci, A. (1992). *Prison Notebooks*. Columbia University Press.

Greenfeld, L. (2019). *Nationalism: A Short History*. Brookings Institution Press.

Grobe, C. (2020). The artist is President: Performance art and other keywords in the age of Donald Trump. *Critical Inquiry*, 46(4), 764–805.

Gutierrez, N. (2018). Indigenous myths and nation building in Latin America: Ethnicity and nationalisms. *Nations and Nationalism*, 24(2), 271–80. https://doi.org/10.1111/nana.12387

Habermas, J. (1991). *The Structural Transformation of the Public Sphere: An Inquiry into a Category of Bourgeois Society*. MIT Press.

Habermas, J. (2007 [1981]). *Reason and the Rationalization of Society*. Beacon Press.

Habermas, J. (2012). *The Crisis of the European Union: A Response*, trans. C. Cronin. Polity.

Hage, G. (2017). *Is Racism an Environmental Threat?* Polity.

Hall, S.M. (2018). Migrant margins: The streetlife of discrimination. *The Sociological Review*, 66(5), 968–83.

Hall, S.M. (2021). *The Migrant's Paradox: Street Livelihoods and Marginal Citizenship in Britain*. University of Minnesota Press.

Hammett, D. & Jackson, L. (2018). Developing a 'civil' society in partial democracies: In/civility and a critical public sphere in Uganda and Singapore. *Political Geography*, 67, 145–55.

Han, C. (2018). Precarity, precariousness, and vulnerability. *Annual Review of Anthropology*, 47, 331–43. https://doi.org/10.1146/annurev-anthro-102116-041644

Hanieh, A. (2021). Petrochemical empire: The geo-politics of fossil-fuelled production. *New Left Review*, 130, 25–51.

Hansen, P. & Jonsson, S. (2014). *Eurafrica: The Untold History of European Integration and Colonialism*. Bloomsbury.

Hansen, P. & Jonsson, S. (2017). Eurafrica incognita: The colonial origins of the European Union. *History of the Present*, 7(1), 1–32.

Haraway, D.J. (2016). *Staying with the Trouble: Making Kin in the Chthulucene*. Duke University Press.

Hartmann, S. (2019). *Wayward Lives, Beautiful Experiments*. Serpent's Tail.

Hawthorne, C. (2017). In search of Black Italia. *Transition*, 123, 152–74.

Hébert, K. (2016). Chronicle of a disaster foretold: Scientific risk assessment, public participation, and the politics of imperilment in Bristol Bay, Alaska. *Journal of the Royal Anthropological Institute*, 22(S1), 108–26. https://doi.org/10.1111/1467-9655.12396

Hendrickson, C.J. (2018). The European Project and its enemies. In Galston, W.A., *Anti-Pluralism: The Populist Threat to Liberal Democracy* (pp. 41–63). Yale University Press.

Hernández Burgos, C. (2021). Nationalisation, banal nationalism and everyday nationhood in a dictatorship: The Franco regime in Spain. *Nations and Nationalism*, 27(3), 690–704. https://doi.org/10.1111/nana.12621

Hochschild, A.R. (2018). *Strangers in Their Own Land: Anger and Mourning on the American Right*. The New Press.

Holst, C. & Molander, A. (2018). Asymmetry, disagreement and biases: Epistemic worries about expertise. *Social Epistemology*, 32(6), 358–71. https://doi.org/10.1080/02691728.2018.1546348

Hook, D. (2017). The Mandela imaginary. In M. van Bever Donker, R. Truscott, G. Minkley & P. Lalu (Eds.), *Remains of the Social: Desiring the Post-Apartheid* (pp. 40–64). Wits University Press.

Illeris, H. (2015). 'Just building': Togetherness as art and education in a Copenhagen neighborhood. *Visual Arts Research*, 41(1), 67–83. https://doi.org/10.5406/visuartsrese.41.1.0067

Jacoby, R. (2005). *Picture Imperfect: Utopian Thought for an anti-Utopian Age*. Columbia University Press.

Jacquet, V. (2017). Explaining non-participation in deliberative minipublics. *European Journal of Political Research*, 56(3), 640–59. https://doi.org/10.1111/1475-6765.12195

Jacquet, V. (2019). The role and the future of deliberative minipublics: A citizen perspective. *Political Studies*, 67(3), 639–57. https://doi.org/10.1177/0032321718794358

Jasanoff, S. (2011). Cosmopolitan knowledge: Climate science and global civic epistemology. In J.S. Dryzek, R.B. Norgaard & D. Schlosberg (Eds.), *The Oxford Handbook of Climate Change and Society*. Oxford University Press.

Jasanoff, S. & Simmet, H.R. (2017). No funeral bells: Public reason in a 'post-truth' age. *Social Studies of Science*, 47(5), 751–70. https://doi.org/10.1177/0306312717731936

Jensen, L. (Ed.). (2016). *The Roots of Nationalism: National Identity Formation in Early Modern Europe, 1600–1815*. Amsterdam University Press.

Kallis, A. (2018). The European Union and the mainstreaming of the radical right. *Insight Turkey*, 20(3), 61–76.

Kapila, S. (2021). *Violent Fraternity: Indian Political Thought in the Global Age*. Princeton University Press.

Kelly, A.H. & Lezaun, J. (2017). The wild indoors: Room-spaces of scientific inquiry. *Cultural Anthropology*, 32(3), 367–98.

Kelly, A.H. & McGoey, L. (2018). Facts, power and global evidence: A new empire of truth. *Economy and Society*, 47(1), 1–26. https://doi.org/10.1080/03085147.2018.1457261

Kennedy, J. (2018). *Authentocrats: Culture, Politics and the New Seriousness*. Watkins Media Limited.

Kindersley, N. (2019). Rule of whose law? The geography of authority in Juba, South Sudan. *The Journal of Modern African Studies*, 57(1), 61–83.

Kishore, S. (2019). At the crossroads of the body and the word: Interrogating culture through a performance paradigm. *SAGE Open*, 9(2). https://doi.org/10.1177/2158244019846684

Klug, B. (2017). A world of difference. In A. Lerman (Ed.), *Do I Belong?* (pp. 116–30). Pluto Press.

Koritz, A. & Sanchez, G.J. (2009). Introduction. In A. Koritz & G.J. Sanchez (Eds.), *Civic Engagement in the Wake of Katrina* (pp. 19–22). University of Michigan Press.

Kovačević, N. (2018). *Uncommon Alliances: Cultural Narratives of Migration in the New Europe*. Edinburgh University Press.

Krastev, I. (2020). The fear of shrinking numbers. *Journal of Democracy*, 31(1), 66–74.

Kruglova, A. (2017). Social theory and everyday Marxists: Russian perspectives on epistemology and ethics. *Comparative Studies in Society and History*, 59(4), 759–85. https://doi.org/10.1017/S0010417517000275

Kulicka, K. (2017). Not refugees but rapists and colonizers: The 'European migration crisis' through object-relation theory. *PhiloSOPHIA*, 7(2), 261–79.

Kunreuther, L. (2018). Sounds of democracy: Performance, protest, and political subjectivity. *Cultural Anthropology*, 33(1), 1–31.

Labanyi, J. (2019). *Spanish Culture from Romanticism to the Present: Structures of Feeling*. Legenda.

Lai, L. & Farquhar, J. (2020). Toward knowing: Engaging Chinese medical worlds. *The Sociological Review*, 68(2), 401–17. https://doi.org/10.1177/0038026120905490

Lalu, P. (2017). The Trojan Horse and the 'Becoming Technical of the Human'. In M. van Bever Donker, R. Truscott, G. Minkley & P. Lalu (Eds.), *Remains of the Social: Desiring the Post-Apartheid* (pp. 249–74). Wits University Press.

Lancione, M. (2019). Weird exoskeletons: Propositional politics and the making of home in underground Bucharest. *International*

Journal of Urban and Regional Research, 43(3), 535–50. https://doi.org/10.1111/1468-2427.12787

Latour, B. (2007). *Reassembling the Social: An Introduction to Actor-Network-Theory*. Oxford University Press.

Latour, B. (2018). *Down to Earth: Politics in the New Climatic Regime*, trans. C. Porter. Polity.

Latour, B. & Lenton, T.M. (2019). Extending the domain of freedom, or why Gaia is so hard to understand. *Critical Inquiry*, 45(3), 659–80. https://doi.org/10.1086/702611

Latour, B. & Weibel, P. (Eds.). (2005). *Making Things Public: Atmospheres of Democracy*. MIT Press.

Latour, B., Schaffer, S. & Gagliardi, P. (2020). *A Book of the Body Politic: Connecting Biology, Politics, and Social Theory*. Cini Foundation.

Lee, P.S.N., So, C.Y.K., Lee, F., Leung, L. & Chan, M. (2018). Social media and political partisanship – A subaltern public sphere's role in democracy. *Telematics and Informatics*, 35(7), 1949–57. https://doi.org/10.1016/j.tele.2018.06.007

Lee, R.L.M. (2016). Smart swarms: Some observations on contagion and cohesion in cell-phone society. *Distinktion: Journal of Social Theory*, 17(1), 109–19. https://doi.org/10.1080/1600910X.2015.1068202

Lee, R.L.M. (2017). Do online crowds really exist? Proximity, connectivity and collectivity. *Distinktion: Journal of Social Theory*, 18(1), 82–94. https://doi.org/10.1080/1600910X.2016.1218903

Lidskog, R. & Standring, A. (2020). The institutional machinery of expertise: Producing facts, figures and futures in COVID-19. *Acta Sociologica*, 63(4), 443–6. https://doi.org/10.1177/0001699320961807

Lindaman, D. (2017). Cine-cartography: The cinematic in Paul Vidal de la Blache. *Nineteenth-Century French Studies*, 46(1–2), 114–27.

Lizárraga, F.A. (2021). Equality, liberty, and fraternity: The relevance of Edward Bellamy's utopia for contemporary political theory. *Utopian Studies*, 31(3), 512–31. https://doi.org/10.5325/utopianstudies.31.3.0512

Lucassen, L. & Lucassen, J. (2015). The strange death of Dutch tolerance: The timing and nature of the pessimist turn in the Dutch migration debate. *The Journal of Modern History*, 87(1), 72–101. https://doi.org/10.1086/681211

MacClancy, J. (2016). Down with identity! Long live humanity! In T.H. Eriksen & E. Schober (Eds.), *Identity Destabilised* (pp. 20–41). Pluto Press.

Maliniak, D., Parajon, E. & Powers, R. (2021). Epistemic communities and public support for the Paris Agreement on Climate Change. *Political Research Quarterly*, 74(4), 866–81. https://doi.org/10.1177/1065912920946400

Malm, A. (2018). *The Progress of this Storm: Nature and Society in a Warming World*. Verso.

Martin, D. (2019). Endotic Englishness: In C. Forsdick, A. Leak & R. Phillips (Eds.), *Georges Perec's Geographies* (pp. 186–99). UCL Press.

Massey, D. (2005). *For Space*. Sage.

Mbembe, A. (2021). *Out of the Dark Night*. Columbia University Press.

McFarlane, C. (2021). *Fragments of the City: Making and Remaking Urban Worlds*. University of California Press.

McGilchrist, I. (2019). *The Master and His Emissary: The Divided Brain and the Making of the Western World*, new exp. edn. Yale University Press.

Mehta, M.G. (2017). From Gandhi to gurus: The rise of the 'gurusphere'. *South Asia: Journal of South Asian Studies*, 40(3), 500–16. https://doi.org/10.1080/00856401.2017.1302047

Mendes-Flohr, P. (2019). *Martin Buber*. Yale University Press.

Merrill, H. (2015). In other wor(l)ds: Situated intersectionality in Italy. In H. Merrill & L.M. Hoffman (Eds.), *Spaces of Danger: Culture and Power in the Everyday* (pp. 77–102). University of Georgia Press.

Miller, M.L. (2017). Figuring Blackness in a place without race: Sweden, recently. *ELH*, 84(2), 377–97.

Mishra, P. (2017). *Age of Anger: A History of the Present*. Farrar, Straus and Giroux.

Mitchell, L. (2018). Civility and collective action: Soft speech, loud roars, and the politics of recognition. *Anthropological Theory*, 18(2–3), 217–47. https://doi.org/10.1177/1463499618782792

Mitchell, W. (2021). Present tense 2020: An iconology of the epoch. *Critical Inquiry*, 47(2), 370–406.

Mlekuž, J. (2020). The renaissance of sausage: The role of Kranjska sausage in the contemporary process of reconstructing the Slovenian nation. *Nations and Nationalism*, 26(2), 407–23. https://doi.org/10.1111/nana.12572

Modood, T. (2018). Interculturalism: Not a new policy paradigm. *Comparative Migration Studies*, 6(1), 1–8.

Monbiot, G. (2017). Neoliberalism: The deep story that lies beneath Donald Trump's triumph. *New Agenda: South African Journal of Social and Economic Policy*, 2017(65), 34–35.

Moore, A. (2021). Three models of democratic expertise. *Perspectives on Politics*, 19(2), 553–63. https://doi.org/10.1017/S1537592720002480

Morton, T. (2013). *Hyperobjects: Philosophy and Ecology after the End of the World*. University of Minnesota Press.

Moten, F. (2018). *Stolen Life*. Duke University Press.

Mouffe, C. (1999). Deliberative democracy or agonistic pluralism? *Social Research*, 66(3), 745–58.

Mufti, A. R. (2007). Fanatics in Europa. *Boundary 2*, 34(1), 17–23.

Nancy, J.-L. (2000). *Being Singular Plural*. Stanford University Press.

Nash, J.C. (2018). *Black Feminism Reimagined*. Duke University Press.

Nayak, A. (2003). Last of the 'real Geordies'? White masculinities and the subcultural response to deindustrialisation. *Environment and Planning D: Society and Space*, 21(1), 7–25. https://doi.org/10.1068/d44j

Nayak, A. (2017). Purging the nation: Race, conviviality and embodied encounters in the lives of British Bangladeshi Muslim young women. *Transactions of the Institute of British Geographers*, 42(2), 289–302. https://doi.org/10.1111/tran.12168

N'Guessan, K., Lentz, C. & Gabriel, M.-C. (2017). Performing the national territory: The geography of national-day celebrations. *Nations and Nationalism*, 23(4), 686–706. https://doi.org/10.11 11/nana.12332

Noonan, J. (2019). Paul Virilio and the temporal conditions of philosophical thinking. *Time & Society*, 28(2), 763–82. https://doi.org /10.1177/0961463X17701957

Norton, C. & Donnelly, M. (2016). Thinking the past politically: Palestine, power and pedagogy. *Rethinking History*, 20(2), 192–216. https://doi.org/10.1080/13642529.2016.1153307

Nyong'o, T. (2018). *Afro-Fabulations*. New York University Press.

O'Brien, P. (2016). *The Muslim Question in Europe: Political Controversies and Public Philosophies*. Temple University Press.

Oliart, P. & Triquell, A. (2019). Photography collectives and anti-racism in Peru and Argentina. In P. Wade, J. Scorer & I. Aguiló (Eds.), *Cultures of Anti-Racism in Latin America and the Caribbean* (pp. 49–72). University of London Press.

O'Neill, O. (2002). *A Question of Trust: The BBC Reith Lectures 2002*. Cambridge University Press.

O'Neill, O. (2018). Linking trust to trustworthiness. *International Journal of Philosophical Studies*, 26(2), 293–300. https://doi.org /10.1080/09672559.2018.1454637

Oreskes, N. & Conway, E.M. (2010). *Merchants of Doubt: How a Handful of Scientists Obscured the Truth on Issues from Tobacco Smoke to Global Warming*. Bloomsbury Press.

Orwell, G. (2018 [1945]). *Notes on Nationalism*. Penguin Classics.

Page, J. (2021). *Decolonizing Science in Latin American Art*. UCL Press.

Palmer, J., Owens, S. & Doubleday, R. (2019). Perfecting the 'elevator pitch'? Expert advice as locally-situated boundary work. *Science and Public Policy*, 46(2), 244–53. https://doi.org/10.1093/scipol /scy054

Pearl, J. (2019). Aerostatic bodies and the view from above in late eighteenth-century Britain. *Studies in Eighteenth-Century Culture*, 48(1), 117–38. https://doi.org/10.1353/sec.2019.0009

Pettersson, K., Liebkind, K. & Sakki, I. (2016). You who are an immigrant – Why are you in the Sweden Democrats? *Discourse & Society*, 27(6), 624–41.

Polyakova, A. & Fligstein, N. (2016). Is European integration causing Europe to become more nationalist? Evidence from the 2007–9 financial crisis. *Journal of European Public Policy*, 23(1), 60–83. https://doi.org/10.1080/13501763.2015.1080286

Press, R. (2017). Dangerous crossings: Voices from the African migration to Italy/Europe. *Africa Today*, 64(1), 3–27.

Prvački, A.I. (2020). Reclaimed civility. In I. Aristarkhova, *Arrested Welcome: Hospitality in Contemporary Art* (pp. 1–28). University of Minnesota Press.

Radin, J. (2019). Alternative facts and states of fear: Reality and STS in an age of climate fictions. *Minerva*, 57(4), 411–31. https://doi.org/10.1007/s11024-019-09374-5

Raheb, V. (2017). A never-ending story. In A. Lerman (Ed.), *Do I Belong?* (pp. 131–43). Pluto Press.

Raussert, W. (2018). Sounds of freedom, cosmopolitan democracy, and shifting cultural politics: In H. Bak, F. Mehring & M. Roza (Eds.), *Politics and Cultures of Liberation* (Vol. 7, pp. 192–208). Brill.

Rechtman, R. (2017). From an ethnography of the everyday to writing echoes of suffering. *Medicine Anthropology Theory*, 4(3), 130–42. https://doi.org/10.17157/mat.4.3.474

Richaud, L. & Amin, A. (2020). Life amidst rubble: Migrant mental health and the management of subjectivity in urban China. *Public Culture*, 32(1), 77–106. https://doi.org/10.1215/08992363-7816305

Rieder, B. (2020). *Engines of Order: A Mechanology of Algorithmic Techniques*. Amsterdam University Press.

Rogaly, B. (2020). *Stories from a Migrant City: Living and Working together in the Shadow of Brexit*. Manchester University Press.

Rose, N. & Fitzgerald, D. (2022). *The Urban Brain: Mental Health in the Vital City*. Princeton University Press.

Rowley, D.G. (2012). Giuseppe Mazzini and the democratic logic of nationalism. *Nations and Nationalism*, 18(1), 39–56. https://doi.org/10.1111/j.1469-8129.2011.00501.x

Ruchel-Stockmans, K. (2021). From amateur video to new documentary formats: Citizen journalism and a reconfiguring of historical knowledge. In A. Strohmaier & A. Krewani (Eds.), *Media and Mapping Practices in the Middle East and North Africa: Producing Space* (pp. 139–58). Amsterdam University Press.

Schiller, D. (2020). Reconstructing public utility networks: A program for action. *International Journal of Communication*, 14, 4989–5000.

Schlesinger, P. (2020). After the post-public sphere. *Media, Culture & Society*, 42(7–8), 1545–63. https://doi.org/10.1177/0163443720948003

Schmitt-Beck, R. & Grill, C. (2020). From the living room to the meeting hall? Citizens' political talk in the deliberative system. *Political Communication*, 37(6), 832–51. https://doi.org/10.1080/10584609.2020.1760974

Scruton, R. (2018). The open society from a conservative perspective. In M. Ignatieff & S. Roch (Eds.), *Rethinking Open Society* (pp. 31–46). Central European University Press.

Sethi, A. (2012). *A Free Man: A True Story of Life and Death in Delhi*. W.W. Norton & Company.

Sha, S. & Quet, M. (2020). From expression to expulsion: Digital public spaces as theatres of operations in Nepal. *Science, Technology and Society*, 25(3), 386–403. https://doi.org/10.1177/0971721820912896

Shapin, S. (2019). Why was 'custom a second nature' in early modern medicine? *Bulletin of the History of Medicine*, 93(1), 1–26. https://doi.org/10.1353/bhm.2019.0000

Shroufi, O. (2015). The Gates of Jerusalem: European revisionism and the populist radical right. *Race & Class*, 57(2), 24–42. https://doi.org/10.1177/0306396815595799

Simone, A. (2018). *Improvised Lives: Rhythms of Endurance in an Urban South*. Polity.

Simone, A. (2022) *Surrounds: Urban Life within and beyond Capture*. Duke University Press.

Simpson, P. (2013). Ecologies of experience: Materiality, sociality, and the embodied experience of (street) performing. *Environment and Planning A*, 45(1), 180–96. https://doi.org/10.1068/a4566

Singh, B. (2015). *Poverty and the Quest for Life: Spiritual and Material Striving in Rural India*. University of Chicago Press.

Skinner, Q. (1990). The Republican ideal of political liberty. In G. Bock, Q. Skinner & M. Viroli (Eds.), *Machiavelli and Republicanism* (pp. 293–309). Cambridge University Press.

Slotta, J. (2017). Can the subaltern listen? Self-determination and the provisioning of expertise in Papua New Guinea. *American Ethnologist*, 44(2), 328–40. https://doi.org/10.1111/amet.12482

Slotta, J. (2019). The annotated Donald Trump: Signs of circulation in a time of bubbles. *Journal of Linguistic Anthropology*, 29(3), 397–416. https://doi.org/10.1111/jola.12228

Smith, A.W.M. (2017). African dawn. *Historical Reflections/Réflexions Historiques*, 43(3). https://doi.org/10.3167/hrrh.2017.430306

Smith, S.B. (2019). Patriotism as loyalty. *Social Research: An International Quarterly*, 86(3), 583–605.

Sodaro, A. (2018). *Exhibiting Atrocity: Memorial Museums and the Politics of Past Violence*. Rutgers University Press.

Solnit, R. (2021). Ten ways to confront the climate crisis without losing hope. *The Guardian*, 18 November.

Sorace, C. (2020). Metrics of exceptionality, simulated intimacy. *Critical Inquiry*, 46(3), 555–77.

Spackman, C. (2020). In smell's shadow: Materials and politics at the edge of perception. *Social Studies of Science*, 50(3), 418–39. https://doi.org/10.1177/0306312720918946

Spicer, A. (2017). Iconoclasm. *Renaissance Quarterly*, 70(3), 1007–22.

Stehle, M. & Weber, B. (2020). Conclusion: Precarious intimacies, collaborations, and solidarities. In *Precarious Intimacies* (pp. 145–54). Northwestern University Press.

Stengers, I. (2015a). Accepting the reality of Gaia: A fundamental shift? In C. Hamilton, C. Bonneuil & F. Gemenne (Eds.), *The*

Anthropocene and the Global Environmental Crisis (pp. 134–44). Routledge.

Stengers, I. (2015b). *In Catastrophic Times: Resisting the Coming Barbarism*, trans. A. Goffey. Open Humanities Press/Meson Press.

Sternfeld, N. (2017). Belonging to the contact zone. In A. Lerman (Ed.), *Do I Belong?* (pp. 254–69). Pluto Press.

Stewart, E. & Hartmann, D. (2020). The new structural transformation of the public sphere. *Sociological Theory*, 38(2), 170–91. https://doi.org/10.1177/0735275120926205

Stewart, K. (2011). Atmospheric attunements. *Environment and Planning D: Society and Space*, 29(3), 445–53. https://doi.org/10.1068/d9109

Storm, E. (2017). The nationalisation of the domestic sphere. *Nations and Nationalism*, 23(1), 173–93. https://doi.org/10.1111/nana.12290

Stråth, B. (2017). Identity and social solidarity: An ignored connection. A historical perspective on the state of Europe and its nations. *Nations and Nationalism*, 23(2), 227–47. https://doi.org/10.1111/nana.12299

Strathern, M. (2020). *Relations: An Anthropological Account*. Duke University Press.

Tadiar, N.X.M. (2022). *Remaindered Life*. Duke University Press.

Tamir, Y. (2019). *Why Nationalism*. Princeton University Press.

Tamir, Y. (2020). Why nationalism? Because nothing else works. *Nations and Nationalism*, 26(3), 538–43. https://doi.org/10.1111/nana.12619

Taylor, L. (2020). The price of certainty: How the politics of pandemic data demand an ethics of care. *Big Data & Society*, 7(2), 205395172094253. https://doi.org/10.1177/2053951720942539

Taylor, M. & Mishra, P. (2019). We've moved very far from any realistic notion of democracy. We continue to use these words without realising that they've been hollowed out. *RSA Journal*, 165(3), 24–9.

Thakur, A.K. (2020). New media and the Dalit counter-public sphere. *Television & New Media*, 21(4), 360–75. https://doi.org/10.1177/1527476419872133

Thieme, T. (2018). The hustle economy: Rethinking geographies of informality and getting by. *Progress in Human Geography*, 42(4), 529–48. https://doi.org/10.1177/0309132517690039

Thompson, J.B. (2020). Mediated interaction in the digital age. *Theory, Culture & Society*, 37(1), 3–28. https://doi.org/10.1177/0263276418808592

Triandafyllidou, A. (2020). Nationalism in the 21st century: Neo-tribal or plural? *Nations and Nationalism*, 26(4), 792–806. https://doi.org/10.1111/nana.12650

Tulke, J. (2019). Archiving dissent. In A. McGarry, I. Erhart, H. Eslen-Ziya, O. Jenzen & U. Korkut (Eds.), *The Aesthetics of Global Protest* (pp. 121–40). Amsterdam University Press.

Valluvan, S. (2019). The uses and abuses of class: Left nationalism and the denial of working class multiculture. *The Sociological Review*, 67(1), 36–46. https://doi.org/10.1177/0038026118820295

Van Weyenberg, A. (2019). 'Europe' on display. *Politique Européenne*, 66, 44–71.

Vince, G. (2022). *Nomad Century: How to Survive the Climate Upheaval*. Allen Lane.

Virilio, P. (2012). *The Great Accelerator*. Polity.

Voronka, J. (2016). The politics of 'people with lived experience' experiential authority and the risks of strategic essentialism. *Philosophy, Psychiatry, & Psychology*, 23(3–4), 189–201. https://doi.org/10.1353/ppp.2016.0017

Walker, D. (2020). Experimenting with institutions in a 21st century age of 'post-truth'. *Geography Compass*, 14(6), e12489. https://doi.org/10.1111/gec3.12489

Warren, C. (2018). *Ontological Terror*. Duke University Press.

Weber, T. (2016). Metaphysics of the common world: Whitehead, Latour, and the modes of existence. *The Journal of Speculative Philosophy*, 30(4), 515–33.

Wegner, P.E. (2020). *Invoking Hope: Theory and Utopia in Dark Times*. University of Minnesota Press.

Wellings, B. & Kenny, M. (2019). Nairn's England and the progressive dilemma: Reappraising Tom Nairn on English nationalism. *Nations and Nationalism*, 25(3), 847–65. https://doi.org/10.1111/nana.12479

Wetzel, D. (2016). Two examples of recent aesthetico-political forms of community. In T. Claviez (Ed.), *The Common Growl: Toward a Poetics of Precarious Community* (pp. 159–74). Fordham University Press.

Wise, A. (2016). Becoming cosmopolitan: Encountering difference in a city of mobile labour. *Journal of Ethnic and Migration Studies*, 42(14), 2289–308.

Withers, D.-M. (2020). The politics of the workshop: Craft, autonomy and women's liberation. *Feminist Theory*, 21(2), 217–34. https://doi.org/10.1177/1464700119859756

Wright, P. (2020). *The Sea View Has Me Again: Uwe Johnson in Sheerness*. Repeater Books.

Wu, G. (2020). The rivalry of spectacle: A Debordian-Lacanian analysis of contemporary Chinese culture. *Critical Inquiry*, 46(3), 627–45.

Yarchi, M., Baden, C. & Kligler-Vilenchik, N. (2021). Political polarization on the digital sphere: A cross-platform, over-time analysis of interactional, positional, and affective polarization on social media. *Political Communication*, 38(1–2), 98–139. https://doi.org/10.1080/10584609.2020.1785067

Ylä-Anttila, T. (2018). Populist knowledge: 'Post-truth' repertoires of contesting epistemic authorities. *European Journal of Cultural and Political Sociology*, 5(4), 356–88.

Young, R.J. (2016). Community and ethnos. In T. Claviez (Ed.), *The Common Growl: Toward a Poetics of Precarious Community* (pp. 17–38). Fordham University Press.

Zeng, M. (2014). Subaltern cosmopolitanism: Concept and approaches. *The Sociological Review*, 62(1), 137–48.

Žižek, S. (2015). The non-existence of Norway. *London Review of Books*, 37, 17.

Zuberi, M.N. (2019). The man on the moon: A semiotic analysis of scopic regimes in Bangladesh. In A. Punathambekar & S. Mohan (Eds.), *Global Digital Cultures: Perspectives from South Asia* (pp. 261–79). University of Michigan Press.

Index

aesthetics of nation 134–6
   aesthetics of breach 149–58
   romantic and civic nationalism 137–49
affliction and affiliation *see* street affinities, Delhi
Africa
   and European colonialism 35, 149
   nationalism 139
   South African apartheid era 101, 143–4
African Americans *see entries beginning* Black
African Italians 29
Afro-Fabulations (Nyong'o) 151
Akbaba, S. 39
Alam, G. 56
alcohol and drug dependency, Delhi 63, 66–7, 69–70, 71, 77, 83–4
algorithms 108–9, 110, 114–15, 116, 118–19
ALLEA (All European Academies) 122

Amin, A. 22
   and Howell, P. 32, 47
   and Richaud, L. 59
Amoore, L. 114–15, 118
Anderson, P. 161
Andrews, L. 120–1
Ansell, A. 102
Arab Spring 112, 153
Arendt, H. 103
Argentina and Peru: theatre and photography projects 152–3
art and literature *see* aesthetics of nation
austerity 12, 19–20, 22–4, 37
Australian Defence League 146–7
authoritarian democracies, civic activism in 105–6

Back, L. 50
   and Sinha, S. 25–6
Bajrang Dal militants, India 64–5, 68, 147
Bangladesh: secular and religious designs 138

Beaman, J. 29
Belgium: citizen juries 107
belonging
  cultural politics of 161–2
  political imaginary of 4
  see also grounds of belonging
Bennett, J. 142
Berlant, L. 34
Bertsou, E. and Caramani, D. 121
Biehl, J. 59, 60
  and Locke, P. 31
Bimber, B. and Gil de Zúñiga, H. 111
Black Lives Matter movement 132
Black musicians 145
Black oppression and resistance 151
'Black Towns' 150, 151
Bolsonaro, J. 12, 14, 18, 36, 40
Boswell, C. 155
Brandmayr, F. 124–5
Brazil 160
  blessings (*bençao*) as ritual of deferential civility 102
  and Bosnia: ethnographies of conflict 31
  see also Bolsonaro, J.
breach, aesthetics of 149–58
Brexit 15, 17, 24, 25, 39–40, 120
Bryant, R. and Knight, D. 50
Buber, M. 140
Buettner, E. 34
Bush, G.W. 145
Butler, J. 150, 159

Caldeira, T. 59
Camporesi, S. et al. 122
Centre for Equity Studies (CES), Delhi, India 56, 84–5

Chatterjee, M. 95, 100–1
Chatterjee, P. 42, 106
Chin, R. 30, 46
China
  Maoist revival 138–9
  mountain-herb healers 128
citizen juries 107
'citizen science' 126
civic activism and public spheres 105–7
'civic epistemologies' 122
civic nationalism and romantic nationalism 137–49
civic patriotism vs customary patriotism 43–5
civic pedagogies 107–8
civility 101–2
Claviez, T. 32
climate crisis 155–6
co-ownership principle of belonging 30–1
colonialism and postcolonial perspective 34–6, 41, 149
  Caribbean 47–8
'composite community in relation', nation as 47–8
conflicts
  ethnographies of 31
  Israel-Palestine 110–11, 122
  Syrian 153
cosmopolitan nationalism 140
counter-knowledges, digital circulation of 111–13, 119–20
counter-narrative of belonging, absence of 16–18
Covid-19 pandemic 18–20, 36, 94–5, 119
  public trust in science 123–4
Cox, R. 161

cultural politics of belonging 161–2

Dalits
  Delhi 55, 61, 65
  online campaign 113
Das, V. 57–8, 92, 93
Davies, M. 112
Davies, W. 108
Davis, A. 108
De Boeck, F. 58–9
De Genova, N. 28
de Jong, J. and Andeweg, B. 104–5
de la Blache, P. 154
Dean, M. 116
Delhi see street affinities
Demossier, M. 35–6
digital unruliness and public sphere 109–19
'direct democracy' 21
Dolan, F. 103
Dommett, K. and Pearce, W. 121
drug dependency see alcohol and drug dependency
Duyvendak, J.W. and Kešić, J. 2

Ekström, A. 5
Elkin-Koren, N. 118
Elsheikh, D. and Lilleker, D. 113
employment, Delhi 61–2, 63, 64, 66, 72, 78, 79
  and education of women 68, 69, 90–1
endotic art 153–6
Erdoğan, R.T. 12, 110
Esguerra, A. 124
Esposito, R. 31, 133
ethic of care 19–20
Europe/EU 17–18, 19, 161
  attitudes to science and expertise 120–2
  colonialism and postcolonial perspective 34–6, 41, 149
  migrants/refugees 27–31, 34–5
  negative perception of EU and rise of far-right 37–42
  progressive, romantic and civic nationalism 139–42
  'subaltern cosmopolitanism' 24–5
expertise, trust in 119–29

far-right see populist/far-right politics
Farrell, H. and Han, H. 132
Fast, D. and Moyer, E. 77
feminism 151–2
Fenton, N. 107–8
Figueiras, R. 105
films 151–2
financial crisis (2008) 19, 25, 37
Finland 111–12
Fitzgerald, D. et al. 60
folk knowledge 112, 119–20, 128
Foucault, M. 137
France 15
  cartographic art 154
  colonial violence, Africa 149
  Muslims/Islam 35–6, 39, 144
  National Front/Rally 39
  second-generation North Africans, Paris 29
Fukuyama, F. 44–5
Furman, I. and Tunç, A. 109–10

García, H. 104
gender/gender relations, Delhi 65–73, 76–7
  see also employment, Delhi

Index

German unification 141
Gillespie, L. 146–7
Gilroy, P. 33–4, 47, 149
Glissant, É. 47
Goffman, E. 116
Goodhart, D. 21
Gramsci, A. 137, 161
Grobe, C. 147–8
grounds of belonging 12–22
   challenges for progressive
      politics 49–50
   lived identities, imagined
      community 22–36
   people's nation, civic nation
      36–49

Habermas, J. 102, 103, 107
Hall, S.M. 26
Hammett, D. and Jackson, L.
   105–6
Han, C. 93
Hansen, P. and Jonsson, S.
   34–5
Hawthorne, C. 29
health, physical and mental
   Covid-19 pandemic 94–5
   Delhi 62, 64, 69, 70–1, 72–3,
      75–6
   alcohol and drug
      dependency 63, 66–7,
      69–70, 71, 77, 83–4
   organized care 82–8
   Sufi shrines 80–2
   folk wisdom and second
      nature expertise 128
Hébert, K. 127
Hendrickson, C. 38, 39
Hindu nationalism/Hindutva
   14–15, 18, 52–3
   Bajrang Dal militants 64–5, 68,
      147

communalist violence and
   bandh (shutdown) 100–1
'Guru-sphere' 102–3
National Register of Citizens
   84, 86–7
Hinduism and community
   support 79–80
Hollande, F. 144
Holst, C. and Molander, A.
   122–3
homeless settlement *see* Yamuna
   Pushta, Delhi
Hume, D. 48–9
Hungary 14, 18, 20, 37–9
   see also Orbán, V.

imagined community 3, 6, 8–11
   lived identities and 22–36
   'improper community' 31–2
India
   civic activism 106–7
   see also Hindu nationalism/
      Hindutva; Hinduism
      and community support;
      street affinities, Delhi
informal settlement *see*
   Kusumpur Pahari, Delhi
The Infraordinary (Perec) 153–4
intelligence, human/algorithmic
   114–16
intelligence sharing, Kusumpur
   Pahari, Delhi 92–3
interdependencies 156–7
intermediaries in public sphere
   104–5
Islam *see* Muslims/Islam
Israel-Palestine conflict 110–11,
   122
IT corporations 117–19
Italy 15, 39, 124–5, 137, 161
   unification 141

Jacquet, V. 107
Jasanoff, S. 122
　and Simmet, H. 123
Jazz Ambassador tours 145
just society 45–7

Kallis, A. 37
Kelly, A.H.
　and Lezaun, J. 126–7
　and McGoey, L. 122
Kennedy, J. 24
Kennedy, J.F. 144
Kishore, S. 147
Klug, B. 30–1
knowledge/counter-knowledges
　digital circulation of 111–12,
　　111–13, 119–20
　public truths and trust in
　　expertise 119–29
Kovačević, N. 34
Krastev, I. 38
Kulicka, K. 27
Kumar, G. 55–6
Kusumpur Pahari, Delhi 53,
　　54–6, 60–1, 89–93
　forbearance forestalled 69–73
　majbuti (inner strength and
　　resolve) 61–5
　shakti (strength and bridging
　　divides) 65–9
Kvinitz, E. 150–1

Labour Party, UK 17
Lai, L. and Farquar, J. 128
Lalu, P. 101
Lancione, M. 59, 77
Landauer, G. 140
Latour, B. 48, 123, 131, 156
Le Pen, M. 12, 15
Lee, P.S.N. et al. 112–13
Lee, R.L.M. 115

'left-behind' 19, 20–2, 24, 39–40
liberal democracies
　counteracting nativism in
　　1–7
　recovered sovereignty and
　　impediments of 13–14
library cataloguing 154–5
Lidskog, R. and Standring, A.
　124
Lindaman, D. 154
literature and art *see* aesthetics of
　nation
literature and science alliances
　125–6

MacClancy, J. 30
machine learning 114–15, 118
majbuti (inner strength and
　resolve) 61–5
Maliniak, D. et al. 121
Martin, D. 153–4
Mbembe, A. 149
Mehta, M. 102–3
Meloni, G. 12, 15
mental and physical health *see*
　health, physical and
　mental
Merrill, H. 29
migrants and minorities 22–31,
　34–6, 39–41
Miller, M.L. 41
Mishra, P. 47
Mitchell, L. 106
Modi, N. 14, 42, 52, 64–5, 84
moral patriotism vs customary
　patriotism 43–5
mosquito study 126–7
Mufti, A.R. 34
Muslims/Islam
　communalist violence, Gujarat
　　100–1

Delhi 55, 64, 65, 81, 84, 86–7
  Sufi shrines 80–2
France 35–6, 39, 144
Netherlands 41

Nancy, J.-L. 31
Nash, J. 151
National Day celebrations 144
National Register of Citizens, India 84, 86–7
nature, interdependencies and environmental art 155–8
Nayak, A. 24, 27
needlepoint panels of Jewish rural life, Poland 150–1
Nepal: Twitter controversy 113–14
Netherlands
  colonial guilt 41
  professional speechwriters 104–5
NGOs, Delhi 56, 69, 74, 75, 82–8, 89, 90–1
Noonan, J. 115–16
Norton, C. and Donnelly, M. 122
Norway 142
  Nation Day celebrations 144
  public trust in government 122–3
Nyong'o, T. 151

Obama, B. 144
O'Brien, P. 46
Occupy movement 132
Orbán, V. 12, 38
Orwell, G. 43, 44
Out of the Dark Night (Mbembe) 149

Page, J. 157
Palmer, J. et al. 124
Papua New Guinea: arts of listening 128
pedagogy of citizenship 107–8
Perec, G. 153–4
Peru and Argentina: theatre and photography projects 152–3
physical and mental health *see* health, physical and mental
place, accommodations of 23–5, 43
Poland 14, 18, 20, 37–9
  needlepoint panels of Jewish rural life 150–1
political economy 162–5
political imaginary of belonging 4
Polyakova, A. and Fligstein, N. 37
populist/far-right politics 12–22
  attitudes to science and expertise 120–2
  challenges for progressive politics 1–7, 49–50, 130–3, 142–3, 158–9, 160–5
  and digital public sphere 109–10, 111–12, 117
  negative perception of EU and rise of 37–42
poverty *see* street affinities, Delhi
Press, R. 28–9
private and public sphere, blurring distinctions between 116–17
pro-democracy campaigns and social media 112–13
professional speechwriters 104–5
'progressive nationalism' 139–40
progressive politics, challenges for 1–7, 49–50, 130–3, 142–3, 158–9, 160–5

public art 29, 152–3
public sphere 97–100
 challenges for progressive politics 130–3
 for 'common practice with others' 4–5
 digital unruliness 109–19
 examples 100–9
 public truths and trust in expertise 119–29
pundits 105

Raheb, V. 29–30
Rechtman, R. 91–2
refugees 27–9
relational perspective 32–4, 36
 'composite community in relation' 47–8
Rhythm Road tours 145
Rogaly, B. 23–4
romantic nationalism and civic nationalism 137–49
Ruchel-Stockmans, K. 153

Scandinavia
 romantic nationalism 141–2
 see also Norway; Sweden
Schiller, D. 118
science and expertise, trust in 119–29
Scruton, R. 43, 44
second nature knowledge 128–9
Sha, S. and Quet, M. 113–14
shakti (strength and bridging divides) 65–9, 76–7
Shapin, S. 128
Sharan, P. 81
Simone, A. 59, 92
Simpson, P. 59–60
Singapore and Uganda, civic activism in 105–6

Singh, B. 59
'singular plural' 31–2
Skinner, Q. 46
Slotta, J. 109, 128
Smith, S.B. 43–5
social composition and differentiated poverty, Delhi 55, 78
social density and topology, Delhi 91–3
social justice 113
social media 109–11, 112–13
 influencers 116
 see also Twitter
social model of economic management 163–5
'somewheres'/'anywheres' 12, 23–5, 39–40
Sorace, C. 138
South African apartheid era 101, 143–4
Spackman, C. 126
Stehle, M. and Weber, B. 151–2
Stengers, I. 125
Stewart, E. and Hartmann, D. 110
Stewart, K. 60
Strathern, M. 32–3
street affinities, Delhi 51–7
 abjection, flight, organized care 73–88
 choreographies of forbearance 60–73
 embodied affliction, contiguous affinity 57–60
 situated affordances 88–93
 summary and conclusion 93–6
street art 152
'subaltern cosmopolitanism' 24–5

Sufi shrines 80–2
Sweden 41, 142
Syrian conflict 153

Tamir, Y. 142
Taylor, L. 118–19
terrestrial politics 48
Thakur, A.K. 113
theatre: Argentina and Peru 152–3
Thieme, T. 59
Thompson, J. 116–17
Trump, D. 12, 14, 18, 36, 40, 109
truth and trust issues 119–29
Tulke, J. 152
Turkey: Twitter and Constitutional Referendum 109–10
Twitter 109–10, 113–14
see also social media

Uganda and Singapore, civic activism in 105–6
UK
 Brexit 15, 17, 24, 25, 39–40, 120
 Chief Scientific Advisors 124
 cosmopolitan nationalism 140
 Covid-19 pandemic 20
 romantic nationalism 142
 wartime propaganda campaigns 104
 working-class communities 23–4

US
 African Americans *see entries beginning* Black
 Constitution 103
 experts and citizens 126, 127–8
 imagery of unity and soft diplomacy 144–5
 MCHM spillage 126
 moral patriotism 43–5
 see also Trump, D.

Valluvan, S. 27
Van Weyenberg, A. 35
Verma, S. 69
Virilio, P. 115

water supply
 contamination, West Virginia 126
 shortage, Delhi 67–8
Wegner, P.E. 50
working-class communities, UK 23–4

Yamuna Pushta, Delhi 53–4, 56, 73–7
 flight/faith 77–82
 organized care 82–8
Yarchi, M. et al. 110–11
Ylä-Antilla, T. 111–12
Young, R. 31

Zeng, M. 24–5
Žižek, S. 27
Zuberi, M. 138